Schöningh

EinFach
Englisch
Unterrichtsmodell

East is East

Edited by
Carmen Mendez

Series Editor:
Hans Kröger

Einzelarbeit

Partnerarbeit

Gruppenarbeit

Unterrichtsgespräch

Schreibauftrag

Hausaufgabe

filmische Präsentation

Projekt, offene Aufgabe

kreative Aufgabe

szenisches Spiel, Rollenspiel

Vorwort

Der Titel der Reihe **EinFach Englisch** verdeutlicht Zielsetzung und Programm zugleich. Einerseits soll Schülerinnen und Schülern auf einfache Art und Weise der Zugang zu klassischen, aber auch neuen literarischen Werken und Filmen ermöglicht werden, andererseits sollen Lehrerinnen und Lehrern in der Praxis erprobte Unterrichtsmodelle angeboten werden, die die wichtigsten methodisch-didaktischen Ansätze ihres Faches Englisch abdecken. Dabei sind die Modelle direkt, ohne langes Einlesen einsetzbar und stellen Unterrichtsarbeit konkret vor. Als besonders hilfreich für die Praxis haben sich dabei folgende Aspekte erwiesen, die für die Gestaltung der Reihe wesentlich sind:

- Überblick über **Figurenkonstellation**, ggf. **Filmszenen** und **Inhalt**
- **Klausuren** mit **Erwartungshorizont**
- **Arbeitsblätter, Tafelbilder** und **Leitfragen** für den Unterricht
- **Piktogramme** als Hinweise auf **Unterrichts-** und **Arbeitsformen**

Das Prinzip der „**Components**" ermöglicht darüber hinaus den variablen Einsatz der Modelle in unterschiedlich konzipierten Unterrichtsreihen. Dabei stehen Machbarkeit und Praxisnähe stets im Vordergrund.

Das vorliegende Modell bezieht sich auf die englischsprachige DVD *East is East*, FilmFour Limited, 2007.

Sprachliche Betreuung: Simone Duxbury-Ziemer

www.schoeningh-schulbuch.de
Schöningh Verlag, Jühenplatz 1–3, 33098 Paderborn

Druck 5 4 3 2 / Jahr 2012 11 10 09
Die letzte Zahl bezeichnet das Jahr dieses Druckes.

Umschlaggestaltung: Jennifer Kirchhof
Druck und Bindung: Media-Print Informationstechnologie GmbH, Paderborn

ISBN 978-3-14-041228-5

Getting started

George: I trying to show you a good way to live. You no English. English people never accepting you. In Islam everyone equal, see? No black man, no white man. All Muslim – special community.

Tariq: I'm not Pakistani. I was born here, I speak English, not Urdu.

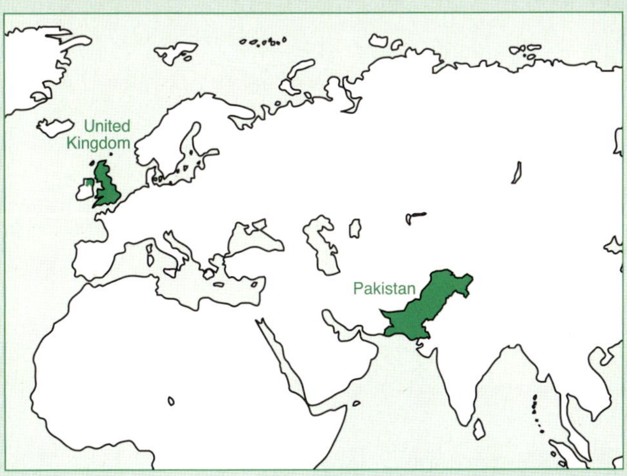

George: I your husband, you should agree with me like a proper Muslim wife.

Ella: I am not gonna stand by and watch you crush them one by one because of your pig bloody ignorance.

Annie: This is religion, Ella, and it's theirs, you know that. You knew when you got married.

George: Pakistani son always show respect. Pakistani believe father ask son marry son follow father instruction.

Tariq: He's never gonna give a shit about how you feel or what you think. 'I'm your father, you are my son, you do as I say!' **Abdul:** I want me family and I don't want anyone hurt any more.

- What image of the film do the DVD-covers convey?
- What issues are dealt with in *East is East* as conveyed by the quotes?
- What impression of the film is created by the quotes?
- Which of the issues are you mostly interested in and would you like to work on in more detail? Why?

East is East

Plot and characters

Plot synopsis

The film *East is East* is based on Ayub Khan-Din's autobiographical play and centres on the problems encountered in a bicultural and interfaith English-Pakistani family living in an overcrowded, red brick terraced house in a white, working-class area of Salford in the early 70s – a political era of growing xenophobia in the United Kingdom.
The film presents the trials and tribulations of George and Ella Khan as they raise eight rebellious children and run a fish 'n' chips shop which barely provides them with enough income to support their family. George, the children's Pakistani father, is determined to ensure that his children are raised in the Pakistani way and marry other Pakistanis, while Ella, George's British wife, would rather their children live their own lives and marry whoever they choose. The children are torn between the strict Islamic dictates and domineering will of their father and the attractions of a secular English life such as discos, pork sausages, modern "Hippie" clothes and football. The central paradox that the Khan children have to face is the fact that their own father chose to marry someone outside his race and culture.
The film raises questions in regard to whether two opposing groups of people from very different cultures can coexist or whether Rudyard Kipling's quote, from which the film (and play) borrow the name, holds true that, "East is east and west is west and never the twain shall meet".

The characters

George Khan (55 years old)
George came to Britain more than twenty-five years ago, probably to earn money for his family in Pakistan. Instead of returning there, he stayed in Britain and started a fish 'n' chips shop that he runs with his second wife, Ella. Even after a lifetime in Britain, George still talks in broken English and uses quite crude language, mostly intermingled with curses such as "bloody" and "bastard". Nevertheless, he remains a devout Muslim and is fiercely proud of his Pakistani heritage and culture. That is why he is so firm in his intent to raise his children as Pakistani Muslims and does not want them to accept the values of Christianity or Western society. To counteract the influence of the English environment, he rules his family with iron discipline. He expects his wife and his children to do what he tells them to do and not to question anything. He is convinced that only he knows what is best for his family and that is why he does not allow any freedom of choice in such an important life decision like marriage. Although the kids try to live by his rules, none of them is able to live up to their father's ideals. Therefore, when his eldest son flees from an arranged marriage, George declares him dead, and when the youngest, Sajid, is found to be uncircumcised, George feels he has to save face with the Mullah and get the "tickle-tackle" done immediately. In one scene, George is shown as a dominant and violent patriarch who loses his temper and beats up both his wife and one of his sons in order to enforce his will on his family.
George wishes his family lived in Bradford, in the Pakistani community, but his wife Ella successfully resists moving there. That is one reason why even George also feels torn between the two cultures. Unfortunately, his own insecurities about his lifestyle make him blind to the needs and conflicts of his children.

Ella Khan (46 years old)

Ella has been the second wife of her Pakistani husband George for about twenty-five years and born him seven children. On the one hand, she consciously keeps up her British identity. For example, she openly revolts whenever George tries to provoke her by threatening to call 'Mrs. Khan number one' – as he calls his first wife in Pakistan – to invite her move to the UK, too. On the other hand, Ella is fully aware of standing in the middle between her husband and her children in trying to reconcile her husband's rigid ways with the needs of her six kids – who nearly all reject the strict values their dad thrusts upon them. Only reluctantly does she accept George's plans and decisions about their children's future as she favours them deciding for themselves on their lives. In some aspects, for example, concerning Saleem's studies and keeping in contact with Nazir, she even goes behind George's back, thus provoking the anger and violence that finally lead her to openly collaborate with her children against her husband.
At first glance, she may not appear very emancipated because, in general, she is loyal to George. However, she knows full well that she is the one who does most of the work in the shop and that she owns the house, which she is prepared to point out to him when talking back and having her equal say. Furthermore, she is strongly aware of George's inner conflict, which is that, even after such a long time in Britain, he must feel as if he is constantly betraying his roots.

Nazir

Nazir is the eldest son, who runs away during his wedding ceremony, thus refusing his father's choice of bride and the edict of matrimony. As a result, he is cut off entirely by George and no longer considered part of the family. In the film, the reason given for his flight is his homosexuality. After the failed wedding, he flees to London, where he starts a new life with a French fashion designer. His brothers and sister come to visit him after an argument with their father but are puzzled by his new life that presents no alternative to them. In contrast to the film, the character of Nazir is not developed in the original play but only mentioned once in connection with the marriage disaster.

Abdul (23 years)

Abdul feels responsible for the whole family and is the only one of the kids working outside the family business. He is also the most passive son and seems prepared to agree to the arranged marriage to make his father happy. Nevertheless, he is a little bit curious about the lifestyle of young English people and thus does not refuse the chance to accompany Tariq to a disco. In the end, he finds it hard to adopt the English lifestyle, and for this reason, neither the young English people nor his colleagues can act as role models for him. It is therefore quite remarkable that it is Abdul who finally stops George from beating up Ella and tells him to leave.

Tariq (21 years)

Tariq is the most strong-willed and rebellious son. In keeping with this, he has adopted a second identity as the English Tony who is allowed to enter the local English disco where immigrants are normally refused. It is Tariq who most strongly imitates the lifestyle of young English people by wearing modern English clothes and having a Beatles haircut. In addition, he has got an English girlfriend, Stella, although it is not clear whether this is truly love or just an expression of Tariq's desire to be more fully integrated into English society. He is the only Khan kid who openly rejects his Pakistani identity, and in keeping with this, he also refuses to accept an arranged marriage with a Pakistani girl. Before reluctantly agreeing to such an arrangement, he holds up a mirror to his father, saying he would like to do things just like him – first marrying a Paki and then an English woman.

Maneer (19 years)

Maneer is the only one of the seven children who does not spurn Islam and their father's world view. He voluntarily goes to the mosque and is the only one who can speak Arabic. Because he never seems to contradict George, he is taken by his brothers and sister to be their father's spy. He is also given the nickname Gandhi whose symbolic meaning is transported in the film when he allows his father to beat him instead of defending himself or betraying his brother Tariq.

Saleem (18 years)
Saleem is the only one whose studies have been financed because George wants him to succeed in British society as an engineer. Instead of studying engineering, however, he does an art course, which he hides from his father. Ella gives him the money for the material he needs for his art. Like Tariq, he wears English clothes and has quite long hair like a "hippie".

Meenah (16 years)
Meenah is the only girl in the family, and contrary to the image of the submissive daughter in Muslim families, she is quite tough, cheeky, and self-confident. Unlike most girls, she plays football with the English boys in the neighbourhood, and Earnest, one of Sajid's young friends, is a big admirer of hers. In general, she is well-assimilated in the English environment. Consequently, she does not like to go to the mosque, nor does she like to wear traditional Pakistani clothes.

Sajid (12 years)
Sajid is the youngest of the Khan children and that is why his siblings always tease him, especially after it is discovered that he wasn't circumcised as a toddler. He is also well-integrated in the English neighbourhood. His best friend is Earnest Moorhouse and he enjoys playing games with the other English kids in the street. When possible, he refuses to go to the mosque and hides from his father, who he is very much afraid of. To protect himself, he always wears a parka that he only takes off at the end of the movie as a sign of self-liberation.

Auntie Annie
Annie, who is called "Auntie" by the Khan children and is like a second mother to them, is Ella's best friend and ally. At this time when mixed-race marriages would have been hardly acceptable and a white woman who married a black man more or less considered a prostitute, Annie tries to support Ella and to defend her against any hostile neighbours. She helps Ella and the children, for example, during the Shahs' visit by pretending to drop by accidentally, then admiring the obviously ugly brides and telling Tariq and Abdul they must be very happy with such a marriage. By showing off an English role model of partnership that Muslims do not agree with, Annie manages to terrify the visitors.

Minor characters are
- Earnest Moorhouse, Sajid's English friend, who admires Meenah and always greets the Khans in Arabic,
- Stella Moorhouse, who is Tariq's English girlfriend and does not care about her grandfather's xenophobia,
- her friend Peggy, who decides to hook up with the unwilling Abdul in order to compete with Stella,
- Mr. Moorhouse, Stella's and Earnest's grandpa, who is a xenophobic neighbour and adherent of Enoch Powell's anti-immigration policy and posts right-wing flyers around the neighbourhood,
- Poppa Khalid, the Muslim imam, who teaches the members of the Muslim community Arabic and religion, and who functions as a match-maker and marriage broker for George Khan,
- the Shahs, a wealthy Pakistani family, who live in Bradford and whose two rather ugly daughters are proposed to George as potential brides for his sons Abdul and Tariq.

Scene index

The scenes are given in order of appearance and with their original titles as listed on the English and German DVDs. (Note the different titles and time spans on these DVDs). This booklet refers primarily to the English DVD as it also offers the option of English subtitles in the menu. However, information on where to find the relevant scenes quickly on the German edition has also been given as a help.

No.	English DVD	No.	German DVD
1	Opening credits Street parade: 00:00–3:01	1	(Vorspann: 00:00) Prozession: 00:20–3:05
2	Proud father: 3:02–9:26	2	Hochzeit: 3:06–10:08
3	Cod & two wives: 9:27–15:09	3	Beschneidung: 10:09–24:29
4	I'll fix him: 15:10–23:05		
5	A good mother: 23:06–27:07	4	Verkuppelung: 24:30–35:39
6	Your daughters are my daughters: 27:08–35:29		
7	A night on the town: 35:30–41:57	5	Kino: 35:40–38:47
8	A right to know: 41:58–45:03	6	Nachtleben: 38:48–45:12
9	Say nothing: 45:04–51:39	7	Vorbereitungen: 45:13–53:52
10	What engagement?: 51:40–59:56	8	Eskalation: 53:53–1:03:38
11	Enough's enough: 59:57–1:05:29		
12	You'll make things worse: 1:05:30–1:08:49	9	Revolte: 1:03:39–1:13:42
13	Show me respect: 1:08:50–1:13:33		
14	Mr Shah's daughters: 1:13:34–1:20:25	10	Familientreffen: 1:13:43–1:23:55
15	The sculpture: 1:20:26–1:23:45		
16	I know what's best: 1:23:46–1:29:50	11	Einsicht: 1:23:56–1:29:59
	End credits: 1:29:51–1:32:15	12	Abspann: 1:30:00–1:32:28

1. Street parade: 00:00–3:01
The film opens with a Catholic procession, the Good Friday Parade. The atmosphere is fun and light-hearted. The Khan children have joined the procession with their English friends and their mother's friend, Annie. Suddenly, Ella Khan appears and warns them that their father George has come back from the mosque. For this reason, the children are forced to detour from the main parade route by taking a parallel street to hide from their father before re-joining the procession later, while George Khan and his wife are greeting the neighbours who are marching in the crowd.

2. Proud father: 3:02–9:26
The setting of the film – Salford, 1971 – is shown and a wall with photos of all the Khan children. The family is preparing for the eldest son's wedding. George Khan is instructing Nazir, giving him a watch with his name in Arabic and telling him how proud he is to be his father. During the ceremony, Nazir is finally shown his bride-to-be, a beautiful girl, for the

first time. Suddenly, he breaks off the ceremony and escapes, leaving his family shocked and totally puzzled. Nazir's picture is symbolically removed from the wall.

3. Cod & two wives: 9:27–15:09
George and the mullah are at the mosque. George thinks he should have moved to Bradford with his family to avoid the disaster at the wedding.
Six months later: The children are playing football in the street. The Catholic priest comes to the Khan's chip shop to collect flowers from Ella and Annie. George enters listening to the latest news from Pakistan on the radio. He makes fun of the priest after he has left the shop. He argues with Ella about providing help for his family in Pakistan but Ella refuses to let George's first wife come over to England. When George sees the mosque's van coming, he rounds up his children and forces them to attend the Koran lesson. With the exception of Maneer, all of them are bored and mostly do not seem to understand the Arabic words. Meanwhile, Abdul stumbles across a workmate's stag party but is left in peace because he does not drink alcohol.

4. I'll fix him: 15:10–23:05
In the mosque yard, the boys have a peeing contest and the mullah discovers that Sajid has not been circumcised. George feels ashamed and accuses his wife of having overlooked this important detail. While the other Khan children clean up the shop, Saleem draws a penis to explain the foreskin's function. Ella and George discuss in a joking tone the necessity of the circumcision and whose house and shop it is. When George mentions his first wife, Ella makes fun of her, doubting whether she would be prepared to do the same hard work in the shop as she does. At the hospital after the operation, George is suspicious because the doctor is Indian. At home, the children are watching Enoch Powell's speech against immigrants while eating bacon and sausages. When they see George coming back with Sajid, they attempt to remove the pork smell. Later, Meenah tears Saleem's drawing of the penis apart to tease Sajid. Later, she dances to Indian music in the courtyard while Maneer cuts up fish and Tariq and Saleem smoke.

5. A good mother: 23:06–27:07
Ella and Annie are at the Khans' house. Ella is stroking Sajid's head since he has now fallen asleep. Ella asks her friend whether she is in fact a good mother because she feels she could have said no to the operation. Annie tells her that she is, but that she also has to accept George's religious beliefs since she knew about them when she married him.
The mullah tells George about Mr Shah and his daughters and he proposes marrying two of the Khan sons off to them to enable the boys to integrate into the Pakistani community more fully. George agrees, and later, when he is back at home with Ella, he first offers her a present – an old barber's chair – and then proposes a trip to Bradford. He does not tell her about his real plans, although she is slightly suspicious.

6. Your daughters are my daughters: 27:08–35:29
George secretly takes two photos of his sons when they go to Bradford or "Bradistan" as a parody of a town sign indicates. In Bradford, Ella meets an English friend who is sad to have let her daughter be married off to Pakistan. Meanwhile, George meets his male friends and Mr Shah. Photos of the potential bridegrooms and brides are passed around. Although George does not seem to be very pleased with the Shah daughters as they are rather ugly, he agrees with the engagement, obviously only to save face.

7. A night on the town: 35:30–41:57
A relative of the Khan family who owns a cinema interrupts a film to show the Khans their favourite film. That night, Tariq and Abdul sneak off from home to go to the local disco

where they are able to enter because Tariq is well-known and liked as his alter-ego Tony. He introduces his brother as his English friend Arthur. Stella and Peggy arrive, too. They all start dancing.

8. A right to know: 41:58–45:03
At home, Ella and George are in bed making love. Sajid enters to pee in his parents' bucket. As he is running out, his anorak string gets caught in the closed door and he overhears his father telling Ella about the engagement. Ella insists that her husband should tell the boys but he does not want her to interfere with his business.

9. Say nothing: 45:04–51:39
In the morning, George warns Ella again to keep silent. At an Asian market, George buys wedding apparel. In the street, Stella asks for Tariq. Her granddad has put Enoch Powell posters at the window. George criticizes his kids for not looking traditional enough. They promise to change their appearance.

10. What engagement?: 51:40–59:56
Ella and the children are talking to Nazir on a public phone while George is watching TV at home. The next day, Meenah plays football in the street and breaks the Moorhouses' window with the Enoch Powell poster in it. At home, the kids chase after Sajid who then tells them about the engagement so that they will leave him in peace. In a rage, Tariq rips open his father's treasure chest, takes everything out and destroys the watches. When George comes home, only Maneer has remained behind. As he refuses to tell his father who did it, George beats him and then takes him to Ella at the chippy. There, he also beats her up because she collaborates with her kids.

11. Enough's enough: 59:57–1:05:29
Intimidated and frustrated, Ella and the children are sitting in the living-room and watching TV. George is still furious and appears frightening to his family. Ella announces the Shahs' visit the following Sunday. Tariq decides to leave and to go to Nazir. Saleem and Meenah join him, as do Stella and Peggy shortly after. Abdul stays behind to please his father.

12. You'll make things worse: 1:05:30–1:08:49
In Eccles, they discover that Nazir is gay and decide not to stay there because his life – completely cut off from the family – is not an option for them. Nazir and his French boyfriend drive them home. Ella sends Nazir away to prevent him from meeting his father and making things worse.

13. Show me respect: 1:08:50–1:13:33
George orders his family to show respect to the Shahs. While Abdul drinks a glass of beer at a pub, he tells his astonished workmates that he is going to be married to a woman that his father has not yet bothered to introduce him to. Tariq, on the other hand, tries to talk to his father about the engagement but George does not intend to change his mind. Instead, he commands Tariq to live up to Pakistani rules. In the end, Tariq gives in, but tells his father he will do the same as him – first marrying a Pakistani and then an English woman.

14. Mr Shah's daughters: 1:13:34–1:20:25
The Shahs arrive in a big, expensive car. Ella and Meenah adapt their language to a more formal accent and word choice to show that they can be at the same level as the rich Shahs. The brides are introduced to their prospective husbands who find it difficult to show any pleasure. The Khans and the Shahs start a conversation about issues such as the proper dress code, discipline and where the two couples will live. Whereas George always agrees with

the Shahs' views even contradicting his former opinions, Ella's reactions show growing anger about the Shahs' posh attitude. During the conversation, Sajid and Meenah leave to look for Saleem.

15. The sculpture: 1:20:26 – 1:23:45

Saleem, who has just come in, proudly presents his sculpture – a model of a vagina that is meant to represent 'female exploitation in art' – to his surprised siblings. When Ella comes to them and sees this 'work of art', she is disgusted and wants to throw it away. This leads to a scuffle with Saleem that ends with the vagina falling into Mrs Shah's lap. The shocked Shahs leave the house with Ella telling them to "piss off" because their daughters would not be good enough for her sons anyway.

16. I know what's best: 1:23:46 – 1:29:50

George is furious and blames Ella for the disaster, who in turn accuses him of being ashamed of her and their kids. When George starts to beat her, Abdul intervenes and pulls them apart. Ella, with all the kids standing behind her in support, tells him to leave. Nevertheless, after they are alone, she takes George's side, reminding the children that he is still their father. Later, she visits George, who is working in the shop, and they reconcile their differences over a cup of tea. Abdul and Sajid decide to throw the parka away since the hood was torn off in the family scuffle earlier. When Saj shows Saleem's 'work of art' to Earnest, Peggy, standing behind, is at first angry since she was the model for it, but soon after, all of them playfully run away down the street.

Biographical information

Ayub Khan-Din (play and screenplay writer)
Ayub Khan-Din grew up in Salford, as one of 10 children to a Pakistani father and British mother. At the age of sixteen, he left school but had severe difficulty with reading and writing. At first, he worked as "the worst hairdresser in Manchester", but after reading David Niven's autobiography *The Moon's a Balloon*, in which Niven writes about his own decision to pursue a career in acting after having served for many years in the army, Khan-Din decided to enrol in Mountview Drama School. Acting thus became his entry ticket to the business, and although he did have success as an actor, Khan-Din feels it was mainly due to his bicultural background, which as he remembers, stamped him with "an invisible mark that said BLACK ACTOR!". Nevertheless, his on-screen credits include the films *My Beautiful Laundrette* and *Sammy and Rosie Get Laid.*
While still at college and in an attempt to understand his past, Khan-Din began writing *East is East*, which is based largely on his own life and experiences growing up in a bicultural, working-class background. The play won several awards and became a stage success – in fact, it was the first ever debut to sell out at London's Royal Court Theatre. Khan-Din later produced it as a screenplay for Miramax films.

Damien O'Donnell (film director)
Damien O'Donnell, born in Dublin, is an Irish film director and writer. He directed *East is East* as his feature-length directorial debut, for which he received a *British Independent Film Awards* nomination. He also directed *Heartlands* in 2002 and *Inside I'm Dancing* in 2004.

Om Puri (George Khan)
Om Puri, who was born in 1950 in India, is a graduate of the Film and Television Institute of India. Since starting his film career in 1976, he has appeared in over 140 films, including mainstream and Indian art cinema films as well as British and American productions. In the course of his career, he has won critical acclaim for his performances in many unconventional roles in Indian films such as a victimized tribal in *Aakrosh* (1980), the leader of a cell of Sikh militants in *Maachis* (1996), and a police inspector in *Aadh Satya* (1982). He has also been awarded the two most prestigious awards that the Indian film industry has to offer. In the mid 1990s, Puri diversified to play character roles in mainstream Hindi cinema, performed as a comedian in Hindi TV serials and earned a reputation as one of Bollywood's greatest. In addition to this, however, he has continued to gain international fame through starring in many British films such as *My Son the Fanatic* (1997), *East is East* (1999) and *The Parole Officer* (2001), acting in Hollywood productions such as *Wolf* (1994) and *The Ghost and the Darkness* (1996) and for his television work such as the Channel Four drama *White Teeth* and *The Canterbury Tales.*

Linda Bassett (Linda Khan)
Although Linda Bassett has been a very successful actress in theatre, television and film productions, she has deliberately kept her private life out of all media publications in order to focus all interest on her professional work. In the course of her career, she has performed at the most important British theatres such as the Royal National Theatre, the Royal Court, the Royal Shakespeare Company, the Theatre Royal Stratford East, and many others. When *East is East* was first put on stage at the Birmingham Repertory Theatre, she played the role of Ella Khan. In addition to her extensive theatre work, she has also been involved in several prize-winning films such as *Calendar Girls* (2003), and *The Hours* (2003).

Ian Aspinall (Nazir Khan)
Ian Aspinall, born in 1971 in Bolton, is a British actor who is best known in the UK for his

role on *Holby City*, where he played Mubbs Hussein from 2001 to 2005. He has also been involved in several TV productions.

Raji James (Abdul Khan)
Raji James was born as Rajesh Jhanji in 1970 in Havant, England. In 1991, he graduated with a Bachelor's Degree from the Royal Welsh College of Music and Drama. In the course of his career, Raji has been involved in a number of TV, film and theatre productions. As an actor, he is best known for his roles in the British soap opera *EastEnders*, as well as in the film *East is East* and in the British TV sitcom *The Office*. He is also a part of a successful and humorous free podcast on the UK Comedy Website, www.chortle.co.uk, alongside the comedians Ray Peacock and Ed Gamble.

Jimi Mistry (Tariq Khan)
Jimi Mistry was born in Yorkshire in 1973 to an Indian father and an Irish Catholic mother. The role of Tariq Khan in the stage production of *East is East* at the Birmingham Repertory Theatre was Mistry's first professional role after graduating from drama school. In his first American film, *The Guru*, he played an Indian dance teacher who moves to America to become a star. Since then, Mistry has gained further exposure by playing a doctor on the British soap opera *EastEnders*, starring in the British comedy *The Truth About Love* and acting in the blockbuster films *Blood Diamond* and *Partition.*

Emil Marwa (Maneer Khan)
Emil Marwa also played the role of Maneer Khan in the original stage production of *East is East* at the Birmingham Repertory Theatre. Television roles since then have included the soap opera *EastEnders* and *Grange Hill.*

Christopher Paul Bisson (Saleem Khan)
Christopher Paul Bisson was born in Manchester in 1975 to an Indo-Trinidadian father and an English mother. Although he first appeared as an actor in 1990, he is best known for his role as Saleem Khan in *East is East*, which he also played on stage, as well as for roles in *Coronation Street* and *Shameless.* In addition, he appeared in the second series of *I'm a Celebrity, Get Me Out of Here!* and more recently, he participated in the Channel 4 Documentary *Empire's Children* (2007) tracing his paternal heritage to the West Indies.

Archie Panjabi (Meenah Khan)
Archie Panjabi was born in London in 1973 and is a Sikh of Punjabi descent. Although she graduated from Brunel University in West London with a degree in Management Studies, she decided to pursue a career as an actress instead. Panjabi has had acting roles in both film and television, including her early appearance in the film *East is East* to the recent BBC television series *Life on Mars.* One of her most high-profile roles was in the 2002 comedy release *Bend it like Beckham.* Her first Hollywood role was as a British diplomat in the Oscar-winning *The Constant Gardener* in 2005. In 2007, Panjabi appeared with Angelina Jolie in the movie adaptation of *A Mighty Heart*, for which she earned *The Chopard Trophy for a Breakout Performance* at the Cannes Film Festival.

Jordan Routledge (Sajid Khan)
There is no biographical information available on the young Jordan Routledge. However, he also appeared in the film *Gabriel and Me*, released in 2001.

Lesley Nicol (Auntie Annie)
Lesley Nicol is a British actress who is most well known for her role as Mrs Beaver in the 1988 BBC adaptation of *The Lion, the Witch and the Wardrobe.* In addition to guest-starring in numerous British television series, she appeared in the West End production of the musical *Mamma Mia!* from 2000 to 2002.

Vorüberlegungen zum Einsatz des Films im Unterricht

Die Behandlung des Films *East is East* ist inzwischen in einzelnen Bundesländern obligatorisch in den Lehrplan der Oberstufe als Analyse eines *feature films* aufgenommen worden, in anderen ist er Gegenstand des Zentralabiturs oder er wird empfohlen.
Es bietet sich an, den Film im Rahmen der Themen *post-war immigration, cultural clashes, integration of second/third generation immigrants* in den Unterricht zu integrieren. Darüber hinaus werden die Themen *traditional and modern role models in families, mixed-race relationships, courtship and marriage, young people* mit angesprochen.
Interkulturelle Bezüge sind mit einer Diskussion der britischen Einwanderungspolitik, der Haltung der britischen Bevölkerung zu gemischtrassigen Ehen sowie der sich in einer bikulturellen Familie ergebenden Probleme vermittelbar. Eine interkulturell vergleichende Reflektion aus deutscher Sicht ist aufgrund des zeitlichen Abstandes der Filmhandlung und der kulturellen Distanz zur pakistanischen Kultur und zum Islam jedoch nur begrenzt zu leisten. Zwar spricht der Film in seiner Mischung aus Drama und Komödie das Publikum, eingeschlossen das deutsche, zweifellos an, diese Stärke des Films aber trägt zugleich dazu bei, einzelne Aspekte wie Fremdenfeindlichkeit, Rassismus und Gewalt in der Familie harmlos erscheinen zu lassen – was in etlichen Filmrezensionen kritisch angemerkt worden ist. Bei Schülern kann daher ein in der Regel recht voreingenommenes und schematisch vereinfachendes Bild von islamischen Kulturen bestärkt werden, welches die Lehrkraft u. a. mithilfe der im Heft angebotenen zusätzlichen Materialien entsprechend zu korrigieren versuchen sollte. Der in Teilen slapstickhafte Charakter des Films sollte allerdings kein Grund sein, ihn nicht einzusetzen, sondern es bietet sich im Rahmen einer Diskussion des Filmgenres und der Werbestrategie für den Film an, diesen Aspekt kritisch-konstruktiv zu thematisieren.

Die im Heft vorgeschlagenen Unterrichtsbausteine versuchen in ihrer thematischen und methodischen Vielfalt den jeweiligen Anforderungen in den Bundesländern gerecht zu werden und ein Angebot zu unterbreiten, welches eine variable Auswahl an Materialien und die Konzeption eines eigenen passenden Unterrichtsmodells zulässt. Es wird dabei vorausgesetzt, dass Grundkenntnisse der Filmanalyse bzw. Materialien dazu vorhanden sind. Wird eine solche Analyse nicht im Oberstufenlehrplan gefordert, so können die betreffenden Arbeitsaufträge in den *Components* unkompliziert gekürzt werden, um sich ausschließlich auf die Inhalte konzentrieren zu können.

Für den Einsatz im Unterricht ist die englische Originalausgabe der DVD zu empfehlen, da auf ihr englische Untertitel einblendbar sind, die sich aufgrund der umgangssprachlichen Verwendung des Englischen und eines *non-standard vocabulary* des besseren Verständnisses wegen anbieten.

Klausuren

Nachfolgend werden zwei Klausurvorschläge unterbreitet, die nach Bearbeitung des Unterrichtsmodells bzw. einzelner *Components* eingesetzt werden können. **Klausur 1** ist eine Film- und Filmgenreanalyse unter Einbezug von Film- und Textausschnitten. Die Klausur ist bei entsprechend flexibler Handhabung des Erwartungshorizonts sowohl in einem Grund- als auch in einem Leistungskurs einsetzbar. **Klausur 2** ist eine Textklausur, welche die Themen Immigration und Integration aufgreift, sich aber nicht unmittelbar auf den Film selbst bezieht. Klausur 2 ist für einen Leistungskurs konzipiert.

Klausur 1 zielt auf eine recht komplexe Untersuchung, inwieweit die kritischen Themen des Films im gewählten Filmgenre in seiner Mischung aus bikultureller Komödie und Familiendrama eine adäquate Form der Umsetzung gefunden haben. Jeweils ein Textausschnitt aus einem Interview mit dem Regisseur sowie kontrastiv dazu aus einer Filmkritik sollen hier in Bezug auf drei kurze Filmsequenzen, aus denen vier Standbilder zur Verfügung gestellt werden, in ihren Aussagen und ihrer Wirkung analysiert und bewertet werden.
Sequenzen:

- Englische DVD: Nr. 10 „What engagement?": 0:53:43–0:57:54
- Deutsche DVD: Nr. 8 „Eskalation": 0:53:53–0:57:50

Die Textausschnitte und Aufgaben sollten zuerst gelesen werden, um die Aufmerksamkeit auf die relevanten Stellen des Filmausschnitts zu lenken. Der Filmausschnitt sollte dann zweimal, möglichst einmal zu Beginn der Klausur und einmal nach etwa 20 bis 30 Minuten, gezeigt werden, damit die Schülerinnen und Schüler sich nach einer Einarbeitungsphase zielgerichteter auf Details konzentrieren können.

Klausur 2 stellt die gelungene Integrationsgeschichte einer bikulturellen britisch-indischen Familie aus der Sicht von drei Generationen dar. Der Text schreibt sozusagen die Integrationsgeschichte der im Film dargestellten Familie Khan im 21. Jahrhundert fort. Vor der Klausur sollten Aspekte der Immigration nach Großbritannien, wie sie zum Beispiel in den *Components 3* und *4* vorgeschlagen werden, behandelt werden. *Copy 11* (S. 68), welche die im Text thematisierte Familie Mattani in Bildern und Zitaten vorstellt, kann mit den entsprechenden Assignments auf die Klausur einstimmen und sie inhaltlich vorbereiten. Diese Vorlage könnte aber auch nach der Klausur den Schlusspunkt der Unterrichtsreihe setzen.

Between humour and dramatic action

The film portrays its characters' ambiguities in part by oscillating between humour and dramatic action, creating a problem of labelling the project according to conventional film genres. O'Donnell says, "We're dealing with racism. We're dealing with the tension between Indian and Pakistani, but we do it in the film with humour because I think that's a great way to make a point. I wouldn't want to see a heavy film about these topics." *(73 words)*

From an interview with Damien O'Donnell (director), 2000, www.popmatters.com/film/reviews/e/east-is-east.shtml

to oscillate ['ɒsɪˌleit] to move between

East is East enters a dark territory when it deals with abuse. In one particularly wrenching scene, we see George lose his temper and beat both his wife and one of his sons. The incident is presented in a far less graphic manner than similar events in other movies, but it is no less disturbing. To balance out grim sequences like this, the filmmakers have leavened the storyline with moments of comedy, some of which are a little too over-the-top and slap-sticky. The most overt of these, while admittedly funny, seem a little forced, as if O'Donnell and Khan-Din believed the only way to alleviate the tension was to do something so outrageous that the audience would have to laugh. *(120 words)*

James Berardinelli, 2000, www.popmatters.com/film/reviews/e/east-is-east.shtml

wrenching ['rentʃiŋ] distressing
to leaven ['levn] to lighten up
over-the-top exaggerated, not realistic
slap-stick type of humour based on simple actions
to alleviate [ə'li:vieɪt] to make less painful

Assignments

1. Considering the basic themes and the historical context of the film *East is East*, describe what happens in the film scenes given. (Comprehension)
2. Analyse what film-making techniques are used to move between humour and drama. What is the function of such a mix in the scenes? Include the additional stills from the film in your analysis. (Analysis)
3. Evaluate the excerpts from the two film reviews with reference to the film scenes. Do you think the serious issues of the film are adequately realized? Justify your answer. (Comment)

Film stills

Still 1

Still 2

Still 3

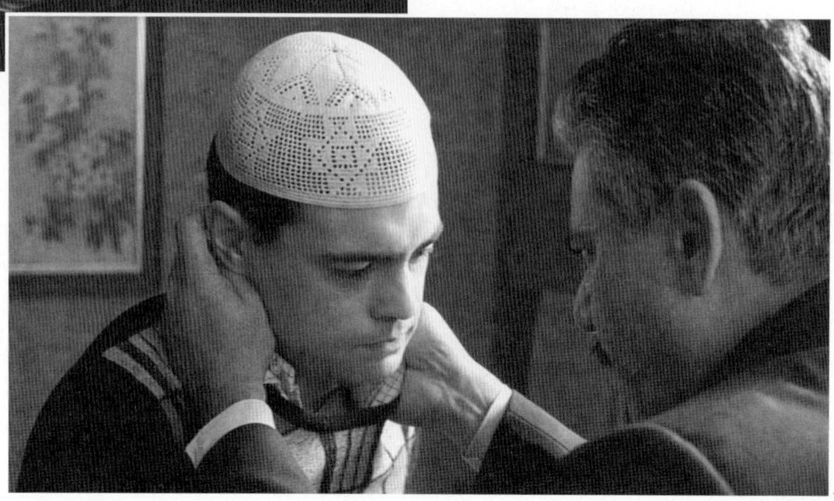

Still 4

Erwartungshorizont zu Klausur 1

Es ist von den Schülern nicht zu erwarten, dass sie den hier gegebenen ausführlichen Erwartungshorizont vollständig bei einer Arbeitszeit von 90 Minuten erfüllen. Die Modellantworten sind daher nur beispielhaft zu verstehen und müssen entsprechend den Anforderungen und Erwartungen an den Kurs angewandt werden.

zu 1: Die Inhalte der Sequenzen werden beschrieben und in den Kontext des Films gesetzt.

Sequences:

- some English children are playing football in the street; Earnest asks Meenah to play with them, who then (accidentally?) shoots at a window with an Enoch Powell poster in it and breaks it
- as all of them run away, Meenah has got a smile in her face, whereas Mr Moorhouse looks out angrily from the hole left in the window
- at the Khans' home, Sajid spies on one of his brothers in order to compare his penis to Saleem's drawing; Meenah calls him a pervert
- a fight starts, which Sajid is only able to escape from by revealing the secret engagement of his two brothers
- shocked and surprised, Tariq opens his father's treasure chest and takes everything out, stamping on and destroying the two gold watches – gifts for the engagement
- Tariq accuses Maneer of having known about it; when they hear their father coming, all run away, except for Maneer who stays behind to tidy up and bear the brunt of his father's anger
- George is furious and wants to know who was involved; he then beats Maneer for not telling him

Context:

- the film takes place in the 70s in the UK at a time when Enoch Powell's policy of repatriating immigrants was supposedly popular, although in the film it does not seem to have many adherents: the majority of the Khans' neighbours are not hostile to the Khan family
- Meenah symbolizes the successful integration of a British-Pakistani girl into British society: unlike an obedient Muslim girl, she wears English clothes and plays football; she is accepted by the English kids in the street as much as all her siblings are
- the real problem is not so much the integration of the second generation of immigrants as the problems that a bicultural origin may bring about within one's own family, which is the main issue of the film as also shown by the scene with George and Maneer

zu 2: Der Operator „analyse" gibt an, dass Filmtechniken im Einzelnen, das heißt zum Beispiel der Bildausschnitt, die Kameraführung, der Kameraschnitt, Requisiten, Ton, Raum und Licht usw., in Bezug auf die Funktion des Wechsels zwischen dramatischen und humoristischen Momenten im Film herausgearbeitet werden sollen. Die vorgegebenen Standbilder müssen in die Antwort einbezogen werden bzw. dienen als deren Grundlage. Die tabellarische Darstellung dient der besseren Übersicht.

Scene/stills	Film-making technique	Humorous effect	Dramatic effect
Earnest invites Meenah, who is passing by with her friends, to play football with him	**Camera:** **establishing shot:** shows the location, the street **medium shots panning** between Earnest and Meenah → **quick cuts** **Close-up of props:** her shoes, football	The whole situation of a younger boy inviting a girl to play with him. Meenah in a skirt, an old football = contrast	
Still 1: The moment after, Meenah has shot the ball into the window	**Close-up:** Earnest's face and Meenah in the background	Meenah smiling → in contrast to Earnest and the other girls	Earnest frightened
All are running away	**Long-shot:** view of the setting – all is empty	Something is going to happen	
Still 2: Enoch Powell poster in the broken window	**Close-up:** window broken and poster torn **Props:** grey colours, poor environment	The hole is exactly where Enoch Powell's head had been on the poster → symbolic action against xenophobia	
Mr Moorhouse	**Close-up** of Moorhouse looking through the hole	Is furious but appears comical	
Meenah, Tariq, Saleem, Sajid, (Maneer) in the house, in Saleem's room	**Cut between medium-shots** of the scene: interaction of siblings **Camera** moving behind Saj, who tries to escape	Meenah and Tariq make fun of Saj's interest in the penis; normal quarrelling	
Still 3: Meenah, Tariq, Saj, Saleem	**Medium-eye-level shot:** all on the bed → neutral, not very dramatic	Meenah, Tariq, Saleem amused	Saj does not feel amused but threatened, promises to tell a secret if they let him go
Saj tells them about the engagement	Slow **music** starts **Quick cut of close-ups** of the faces: shows their reactions		Saj informs about the engagement, Tariq is furious, all are shocked
All go to George's room; Tariq opens the chest; his siblings try to prevent it; Maneer entering	**Low-angle shot** from the chest to Tariq's face **Medium-close-ups** of the other kids to show their interaction Growing **music** till Tariq crushes the watches → danger		Kids try to prevent Tariq from opening the chest and disturbing or destroying anything; they are frightened

Scene/stills	Film-making technique	Humorous effect	Dramatic effect
Maneer alone	**High-angle shot → bird's perspective**, shows the disaster, Maneer appears small and powerless **No music → suspense**		All objects pulled out, the watches destroyed, the obedient Maneer alone
George and Maneer	**Cuts between high-angle shots** of Maneer (helpless) **and low-angle shots** of George (dominant) Maneer with a **white cap** symbolizes Gandhi's peaceful resistance strategy		Shows the dominant father – son relationship; it is not clear whether Maneer will be successful if he does not defend himself
Still 4: George and Maneer	**Close-up** of Maneer's face and a part of George's face **Over-the-shoulder shot** emphasizes George's role as the speaker, Sad **music** starts when George begins to beat Maneer		Maneer: frighten-ed, devout, takes on his brother's guilt; George: furious, domi-nant, violent

Function of the mix between humour and drama:

- the first scene is primarily marked by humour: shows that it is not so much the xenophobia of some British people that makes immigrant families' lives difficult
- British racism is not the main issue for the Khan family; they have learnt to cope with it and do not feel threatened by Enoch Powell's policy nor his adherents like Mr Moorhouse
- more dramatic is the situation within a bicultural family where a patriarchal father does not know how to accept his children's different ways of life and their wishes
- the changes between the humorous and more dramatic scenes show how the Khan children perceive their lives on the one hand
- on the other hand, these film-making techniques enable the viewer to feel empathy and to develop understanding
- if the film did not use humour, viewers would probably not be willing to watch the film; the issue might appear to be too difficult and demanding to cope with and would leave viewers feeling despair and reluctance

zu 3: Der Regisseur und der Filmkritiker vertreten unterschiedliche Auffassungen zum Einsatz komödiantischer Elemente. Diese Auffassungen müssen zunächst benannt werden. Daraufhin wird unter Bezug auf die Filmszenen begründet, ob und inwieweit diese Standpunkte für den Rezipienten nachvollziehbar sind.

Damien O'Donnell:

- problem of labelling: comedy or drama?
- issues: tension between Indian and Pakistani
- does not want a heavy film about these topics; humour is a great way to make a point

James Berardinelli:

- a dark territory when dealing with abuse, e.g. when George beats up his wife and son
- some scenes too slap-sticky and over-the-top, a little forced to alleviate the tension and make the audience laugh

The film scenes given clearly show this alternation between drama and comedy that makes a clear labelling of the film difficult. On the one hand, such a technique does indeed alleviate tension and make the audience laugh. Damien O'Donnell may therefore have been right to have chosen this form of access in dealing with the serious issues of the film in order to attract an audience. On the other hand, however, the critic James Berardinelli also has a point when he criticizes the film as being in part too over-the-top and slap-sticky. Racism and the hostility of the British are hardly mentioned in the film. It seems as if this is not at all important in comparison to the problems within the Khan family. Mr Moorhouse comes across as a comical old man who people can make fun of. It seems doubtful, however, that the situation would really have been that easy for Ella, George's British wife, or that the children would have been so readily accepted in a British environment. It seems far more likely that Damien O'Donnell did not dare to confront a white audience with their prejudices against immigrants. Possibly, he wanted to focus solely on immigrants' problems with their identity, the maintenance of their culture and religion and the issue of integration. If that is truly the case, one cannot expect people to seriously discuss the British contribution to xenophobia.

Barnie Choudhury: Three generations, two cultures

"At the school that I went to in London, there weren't very many Asians so all the other people thought of me as alien, from Mars." [...] Priti Mattani is fortunate. The curious stares and name-calling of teenage school pupils in the late 1970s were her first and only taste of racism in Britain. More than 20 years on, she is married to Hemant and they are parents to two teenage daughters, Shefali, 16, and Nefali, 10. Priti and Hemant both graduated from British universities before going to run the family business in Leicester. [...]

Leicester proved an easy choice of new home for Chandu, [Hemant's father]. Firstly, it was fertile ground for business. Secondly, he could be sure that his culture would not be diluted in one of the emerging centres of British-Indian life. "If I had settled somewhere else where there was no Indian population, I think my children would have grown up in a completely different environment," said Chandu. [...]

fertile [ˈfɜ:taɪl] good
to dilute [daɪˈlu:t] to make a quality weaker

The Mattani family home, now holding three generations, has a relaxed sense of 'let's get on with it without fuss or conflict'. It's a happy home next door to one of the city's golf clubs. The area has a distinctive sense of affluence with BMWs or similar cars parked in most of the drives. For the Mattanis the comfort has come through hard and long hours to make it happen, the Asian way. [...] But the experience of being British with roots elsewhere means the Mattanis celebrate and savour a little of everything that has formed who they are today. "What we've learned is that it's important to take up the good things from all communities and religions," says Hemant. "We'd like to pass that onto our daughters as well."

affluence wealth, being rich
a drive a private road leading from a gate to a house
to savour [ˈseɪvə] to enjoy

So it is hardly surprising that when you broach the question of how Priti met Hemant you get what many would consider an unorthodox response. "We both didn't tell our parents until a time we'd decided that we wanted to get married," Priti laughs.

to broach to mention an embarrassing subject
unorthodox [ʌnˈɔ:θədɒks] unconventional

So you both went behind your parents' backs?

"I didn't," says Hemant, "after a while I did tell my father."

One of the stereotypes of Indian-Britons is the arranged marriage. But it's a custom that has been rapidly fading into history since the mid 1970s. In the case of the Mattanis, the path to happiness was undoubtedly smoother because the two families were already close friends who shared a cultural and religious background.

So what would happen now if Priti and Hemant's own daughters brought home boyfriends from different races, religions or even caste?

"You don't have much choice now," jokes Hemant. "At 12 they threaten to call some of these action lines or parent lines to complain. At 16 they get their provisional driving licences and at 18, they say they're going to do what they're going to do!"

a caste a social class that people are born into in India
action line or parent line telephone line that children or parents can phone to get help

What they have done as parents, he says, is try to show their daughters the right way to take the right decision, whatever that decision may turn out to be. "At the end of the day, it is their decision," he says. "I have seen many cases where parents oppose what their children want and they don't see the other side. And they lose whole links with their children."

Shefali is not so sure that her parents would be so laid back if she chose to go outside her community. "You've got these cultural differences," she says. "Why make your life more difficult? I think they'd prefer it if I was with somebody from my community, or at least Gujarati."

laid-back relaxed
Gujarati [ˌgu:dʒəˈra:ti] name of a language community in India

So where does she place her identity? Does she see herself as any different to other students at her private school? Shefali loves music and films, both Hindi and English. [...] She slips easily between three languages: English, French and Gujarati. "I went to India and I met all my grandparents' relatives," she says. "It was really nice to be able to speak to them, otherwise they wouldn't have understood." [...] While she cherishes her cultural heritage, the idea of staying in a close-knit family and community in Leicester no longer has such appeal. Like so many of her generation, she has her eyes set on university and London. "It's not getting away from my family. It's just that I love

to cherish [ˈtʃerɪʃ] to love sth very much

London. It's more busy and interesting. But I'd like to continue living in an extended family because I like living with my grandparents and mum and dad."

an extended family a big family

In the 25 years since Chandu first set foot in Leicester, the family has seen great improvement in the attitudes between the different races. Today, they find themselves sympathising with Home Secretary David Blunkett when he says that immigrants should sit a citizenship test and be fluent in English. And, at the same time, they see no reason why it means the latest immigrants cannot also hold onto their own culture and mother tongue.

Home Secretary British Government minister in charge of the Home Office, which deals with keeping order in the country

"I'm a British businessman with Indian roots," says Hemant. "My daughter's a British-Indian because the Indian roots are there. It's not something we would want to eradicate. There are good things in there. But this is our home and the first priority is here."

to eradicate [ɪ'rædɪkeɪt] to get rid of

"Both sides are accepting each other more than twenty years ago," he continues. "At that time, white people thought of us as a bunch of immigrants. Now there's a lot more awareness on both sides."

Leicester has long had a reputation for being the model of multiculturalism. [...] "I want to salute Britain," says Chandu. "To accept so many different people, it needed to have something. And that is tolerance and I admire Britain for that. What I say to the Asian communities and everyone is that if you want respect you have to give it. That is my golden rule." *(968 words)*

http://news.bbc.co.uk/hi/english/static/in_depth/uk/2002/race/generations.stm

Assignments

1. Describe the social background of this immigrant family. (Comprehension)
2. Compare the attitudes to marriage and the parent-child-relationship in the three generations. To what extent are these attitudes determined by one's cultural environment and family? (Analysis)
3. What kind of reader is the text intended for? Refer also to the text type. (Analysis)
4. Evaluate the process of immigration and integration that the Mattani family has experienced in the UK. (Analysis/Evaluation/Comment)

Erwartungshorizont zu Klausur 2

zu 1: Die über den gesamten Text verteilten Informationen zum sozialen Hintergrund der Familie müssen zusammengetragen und detailliert in eigenen Worten beschrieben werden. Der einfacheren Vergleichbarkeit wegen werden die betreffenden Textstellen im Folgenden im Originalwortlaut und in Stichpunkten wiedergegeben. Abgeleitete Informationen sind durch Pfeil → gekennzeichnet.

Keywords for the answer:

- the Mattani family home holds three generations: Chandu Mattani, father of Hemant Mattani who has been married to Priti for more than 20 years and who together are the parents of two teenage daughters, Shefali, 16, and Nefali, 10 → traditional extended family
- Priti and Hemant graduated from British universities → high level of education
- afterwards, started to run the family business in Leicester; a British businessman with Indian roots → self-employed, freelance academics with their own business
- a happy home next door to one of the city's golf clubs, an area with a distinctive sense of affluence with BMWs or similar cars parked in most of the drives → wealthy environment, typical (upper) middle-class
- the two families of Hemant and Priti Mattani were close friends and shared a cultural and religious background → the same caste, social status
- from the Gujarati community → all generations have the same background, thus cultural, religious and linguistic identity
- Shefali: at a private school; loves music and films; slips easily between three languages: English, French and Gujarati → a private British school is expensive, so the family must have a high income; the daughter is being educated at a high academic level
- "I went to India and I met all my grandparents' relatives" → keeping contact to their origins, can afford the trip there
- her eyes set on university and London → high aspirations

zu 2: Die Einstellungen der verschiedenen Generationen zu Heirat und Eltern-Kind-Beziehungen müssen herausgearbeitet werden. Von diesem Vergleich ebenso wie von weiteren Textstellen wird abgeleitet, welchen Einfluss Kultur und Familie haben.

Keywords for the answer:

- 1st generation in the UK: Chandu Mattani and (probably) Priti's parents
  - stereotype of the arranged marriage: a fading custom → not decisive in the Mattani family
  - the two families shared a cultural and religious background → shows that the families' backgrounds were nevertheless important and had a significant impact
- 2nd generation: Hemant and Priti Mattani
  - "didn't tell our parents until a time we'd decided that we wanted to get married" → probably had a good relationship to their parents and trusted them, seemed to have been quite sure that they would agree to their marriage; so it seems to have been a self-made marriage with the parents' agreement
  - family has a relaxed sense of 'let's get on with it without fuss or conflict' → harmonious, without aggression, negotiation between the generations
  - parents try "to show their daughters the right way to take the right decision, whatever that decision may turn out to be" → want to help their daughters and

try to teach them "to take up the good things from all communities and religions" as an orientation
- "I have seen many cases where parents oppose what their children want and they don't see the other side. And they lose whole links with their children." → do not want to lose their daughters; know that their British environment has a profound influence on their kids and that parents do not have "much choice now" because of "action lines or parent lines to complain " and other rights

- 3rd generation: Shefali and Nefali Mattani
  - Shefali: not sure that her parents would accept her choice "to go outside her community"
  - knows that there are "cultural differences" → has a very pragmatic attitude when stating: "Why make your life more difficult? I think they'd prefer it if I was with somebody from my community, or at least Gujarati."
  - "cherishes her cultural heritage", "would like to continue living in an extended family" → has a close-knit relationship to her family, does not feel rebellious, would like to live up to her parents' expectations; although influenced by her English environment, Shefali does not want to betray her Indian roots but instead tries to take the best from both cultures → The attitudes of the Mattani family are largely determined by their Indian culture but have also been influenced by the British culture and environment. They show the educated viewpoint of a middle-class family that has been completely integrated into British society without giving up their Indian roots.

zu 3: Die Aufgabe erfordert eine rhetorisch-argumentative Analyse des Textes, um davon die Textsorte und Zielgruppe ableiten und begründen zu können. Die Inhalt-Form-Wirkungsanalyse des Textes wird im Folgenden aus Gründen der Übersichtlichkeit tabellarisch wiedergegeben.

Content (Inhalt)	Rhetorical devices (Form)	Function/effect (Wirkung)
Development of integration from the 70s till the end of the 90s	Detailed description of the integration of the three generations as typical examples	Illustrates the changes in the British society as well as the growing integration and assimilation of immigrants
Marriage: reference to arranged marriages; anecdote of how they met	Arranged marriage, classified as a stereotype, stands in contrast to the decision of the Mattanis	Looks at the typical British or European idea of how Asian marriages are managed, but illustrates that this is a prejudice
Viewpoints of three generations about family life, integration, identity and the achievements of British society	Numerous quotes: "from Mars, curious stares" → "it's important to take up the good things from all communities and religious" → "model of multiculturalism", "I admire Britain"	Shows that the immigrants fully accept the values, rights and laws of British society and are grateful for them; can understand a minimum standard of adaptation such as requiring language skills from immigrants

Text type and reader: The article is a feature story about the integration of immigrants from three generations into British society. The topic is introduced with the example of Priti Mattani's experience of Britain 20 years ago. The text then concentrates on the various members of the Mattani family and how they see themselves and their cultural identity in modern-day Britain. Throughout the article, there is a lot of first-hand reporting to show the authenticity of the example. The article is directed at a typical, educated middle-class readership that is well informed about the successful integration and gratitude of many immigrants. As such, it is probably meant to take away the potential fears of many white English people and reduce their reluctance to immigration, especially in the wake of the terrorist attacks by British Muslims in London and the ongoing discussion on home-grown terrorism in 2001 – 02. Nevertheless, it may be that the author also intends to address readers from different ethnic communities in order to show them a successful example of "multiculturalism" and demonstrate that it is possible to maintain one's cultural and religious origins in a British environment.

---

zu 3: Um den Immigrations- und Integrationsprozess der Familie Mattani bewerten zu können, muss dieser vorab über den Zeitraum von 25 Jahren skizziert werden. Die betreffenden Textstellen werden in eigenen Worten wiedergegeben und kommentiert.

Keywords for the answer:

- 1st generation in the UK: Chandu Mattani and (probably) Priti's parents
  - "white people saw us as a bunch of immigrants" → prejudice, xenophobia
  - "Leicester proved an easy choice of new home for Chandu": good for business, Indian environment → good chance to start a new life in the UK
- 2nd generation: Hemant and Priti Mattani
  - not many Asians at school in London, "people thought of me as alien, from Mars", "curious stares and name-calling of teenage school pupils" → not integrated in the late 1970s but instead open racism
  - Priti and Hemant graduated from British universities before going on to run the family business in Leicester → became successful in terms of education and business; shows growing integration
  - "the comfort has come through hard and long hours to make it happen, the Asian way" → immigrants had to work harder and longer than white people as they had to start from the scratch and to deal with prejudices, even racism
  - "the Mattanis celebrate and savour a little of everything that has formed who they are today ... it's important to take up the good things from all communities and religions" → shows integration and a positive attitude
- 3rd generation: Shefali and Nefali Mattani
  - Shefali "cherishes her cultural heritage", but "the idea of staying in a close-knit family and community in Leicester" does not determine her life, she wants to live and study in London → fully integrated, is similar to British teenagers

→ Chandu sums up the changes he has experienced since he arrived in Leicester:

- great improvement in the attitudes between the different races → positive changes, better acceptance, "a lot more awareness on both sides"
- sympathy with Home Secretary: immigrants should sit a citizenship test and be fluent in English → minimum requirements are necessary for successful integration
- no reason why immigrants cannot hold onto their own culture and mother tongue → important to keep an identity and the "good things" and to be able to assimilate to the western society as the new "home"
- Leicester and Britain, "the model of multiculturalism": "accept many different people ... tolerance" → immigrants should see the positive sides of Britain and be aware of what they should offer, too: "... if you want respect you have to give it. That is my golden rule."

Konzeption des Unterrichtsmodells

Das vorliegende Unterrichtsmodell ist so konzipiert, dass die einzelnen *Components* in chronologischer Reihenfolge, aber weitgehend variabel und abhängig von der individuellen Zielsetzung der Unterrichtsreihe eingesetzt werden können.
Soll der Film vor allem aufgrund seiner Listung als obligatorisches Abiturprüfungsthema ausführlich inhaltlich und filmtechnisch erarbeitet werden, so können alle bzw. Teile aus allen *Components* in der Unterrichtsreihe eingesetzt werden. Es ist dann ein Stundenvolumen von etwa 30 Stunden zu veranschlagen.
Dient der Film hingegen nur als ein Medium zur Erarbeitung oder Ergänzung bestimmter Einzelthemen, so ist der Einsatz ausgesuchter einzelner *Components* möglich. Es wären dann mindestens sechs bis acht Unterrichtsstunden einzuplanen. Die Einsatzmöglichkeiten werden nachfolgend skizziert:

Component 1 führt mithilfe der DVD-Cover und ausgewählter Zitate, welche die im Film dargestellten Probleme einer bikulturellen Familie illustrieren, ein. Die ersten zwei Filmsequenzen veranschaulichen das *Setting* und die Ausgangslage des Konflikts: eine misslungene arrangierte Heirat. Dieser *Component* sollte komplett eingesetzt werden, um ein grundlegendes Verständnis der Filmhandlung zu sichern.

Component 2 enthält Vorschläge für eine *Long-term while-viewing task*, die den Schwerpunkt auf die Charakterisierung einer Filmfigur setzt. Diese Aufgabe bietet sich insbesondere dann an, wenn der Film sozusagen im Schnelldurchlauf behandelt werden soll. Empfohlen sei die im *Component* vorgeschlagene Erarbeitung einer Gegenüberstellung von östlichem und westlichem Kulturkreis in Anlehnung an den Filmtitel. Das Arbeitsblatt *Copy 5* dient der Vertiefung (*attitude to the second wife, circumcision, register*), muss aber nicht zwingend eingesetzt werden.

In ***Component 3*** wird das pakistanische Leben in Bradford dem typisch englischen Leben in Salford gegenübergestellt, welches von den Schülern bewertet werden soll. Dies kann in dichter Form mit dem vorgeschlagenen Tafelbild geschehen. Die Erkenntnisse können mit den bereitgestellten Arbeitsaufträgen, u. a. zur Analyse filmtechnischer Mittel, vertieft werden. Über den Film hinausgehend werden folgende Materialien und Aufgaben zur Behandlung der Einwanderungspolitik und der Situation von Einwanderern in Großbritannien bereitgestellt: Cartoon, Statistiken, Redeauszug aus der *River of Blood Speech* von Enoch Powell, Informationen zur Politik in den 50–70ern, Bradford, Einwanderung heute. Damit deckt der Unterrichtsbaustein eine große Bandbreite an im Abitur geforderten Methoden und Textsorten im Rahmen des Oberthemas *Immigration* ab. Eine Textklausur (2) zum Thema wird angeboten.

Component 4 thematisiert die arrangierte Heirat in Gegenüberstellung zur Liebes- und Zwangsheirat sowie gewalttätiges Verhalten in der Familie zur Durchsetzung von Wertvorstellungen. Vorgeschlagen werden u. a. ein Rollenspiel und die kreative Auseinandersetzung mit einem Text aus einem *Chat-room*, in dem ein unglücklich in einer arrangierten Heirat gebundener Mann um Rat bittet. Je nach Ziel- und Schwerpunktsetzung können nur einzelne Vorschläge aus dem *Component* realisiert werden. Insbesondere dieser Themenkomplex findet aber ungeteiltes Interesse bei den Schülerinnen und Schülern. Die Textklausur (2) berührt auch dieses Thema.

In ***Component 5*** wird detailliertes Arbeitsmaterial zur Filmanalyse mit einem Fokus auf den komödiantischen Elementen sowie auf der Figur des George angeboten. Die Arbeitsaufträge dienen insbesondere noch einmal der Vertiefung von Wissen und analytischer Übung in Vorbereitung der Klausur 1 zur Filmbetrachtung und -analyse.

Component 6 ist ebenfalls optional einsetzbar. Hier werden Vorschläge zur Nachbehandlung des Films gemacht wie z. B. eine Textarbeit zum autobiografischen Hintergrund des Films, die Auswertung einer Filmrezension und das Schreiben eines Drehbuchauszugs.

Von den zwei Klausurvorschlägen ist der erste eine Film- und Filmgenreanalyse unter Einbezug von Text- und Filmausschnitten, wie es in landesspezifischen Abiturrichtlinien gefordert wird. Diese Klausur wird insgesamt im Rahmen der *Components* mit den Beobachtungsaufgaben zum Film, insbesondere aber noch einmal mit einer ähnlichen Aufgabe in *Component 5* vorbereitet. Die zweite Klausur ist eine Textklausur mit thematischer Anbindung an den Film. Wird Klausur 1 eingesetzt, so kann der andere Klausurtext als ergänzendes Material zum in *Component 4* vorgeschlagenen Rollenspiel verwendet werden.

Component 1

Getting into the film

1.1 Getting started

Als Einstieg in die Unterrichtsreihe stellen die Schülerinnen und Schüler anhand der Seite *Getting started* Vermutungen über den Inhalt des Films an: Die DVD-Cover zielen aus werberelevanten Gründen auf eine Vermarktung des Films als Heiratskomödie, was von Kritikern als zu oberflächlich bemängelt worden ist, während die Zitate exemplarisch die Konflikte um Assimilation, Integration und Identitätswahrung in einer bikulturellen Familie in den 70ern im Vereinigten Königreich aufzeigen, was sich thematisch als weniger verkaufsträchtiges Argument geeignet hätte. Dieser Kontrast sollte gemeinsam in einem Unterrichtsgespräch herausgearbeitet und zugleich mit dem im Film behandelten Themenspektrum in einem *Cluster* festgehalten werden, der der Unterrichtseinheit im Folgenden als *Guideline* dienen kann.

Die einzelnen Schritte: Den Schülern wird zunächst die Seite *Getting started* als OHP-Folie präsentiert. Sie beschreiben die darauf abgebildeten DVD-Cover. Die Ergebnisse werden in einem dynamisch zu entwickelnden Tafelbild (und als Hefteintrag) festgehalten. Daraufhin werden die Zitate gelesen und das Tafelbild wird um die Antworten zu den nachfolgenden zwei Fragen ergänzt.

What image of the film do the DVD-covers convey?
What issues are dealt with in *East is East* as conveyed by the quotes?
What impression of the film is created by the quotes?

- marriage comedy: "Das Grauen vor dem Trauen"
- colour pink: symbol of love, innocence, honeymoon
- crude language: "b*ll**cks"
- actors: look amused
- dalmatian dog: reminds one of the cartoon "101 dalmatians"
  → viewers expect a funny film

humorous presentation: to attract viewers

East is East

DVD-cover ↔ **quotes**

about conflicts within a bicultural family such as …
- cultural identity
- religious identity
- wife-husband relationship
- parent-children relationship
- immigration & assimilation → more dramatic

Appealing to you?

Es könnte im Verlaufe des Gespräches eine erste Hypothese aufgestellt werden, warum es zu einer dem Inhalt des Films gegensätzlichen Werbepräsentation gekommen ist:

Why do the covers focus on the comical effect of the film?

Erste Antworten könnten hier bereits gesammelt werden, die später, zum Beispiel mit den *Components 5* und *6*, vertieft werden.
Nach Erarbeitung des Tafelbildes wird kurz diskutiert, welche Themen die Schülerinnen und Schüler am meisten interessieren und aus welchen Gründen.

Which of these issues are you most interested in and which would you like to work on in more detail? Why?

Nach den geäußerten Themenpräferenzen könnte nun die Unterrichtsreihe aufgebaut bzw. ein Projekt entwickelt – und die einzelnen *Components* in diesem Heft – ausgewählt werden.

1.2 Starting to work with the film: Sequence 1 – "Street parade"

Der Einstieg in den Film erfolgt über das Sehen der Anfangssequenz (**En: 0:00–2:47; Deu: 0:00–3:05**). Die Beobachtungsaufträge auf ***Copy 1*** werden vor dem ersten gemeinsamen Sehen gelesen; es ist dabei hilfreich, den Schülern noch einmal die Protagonisten (George, Ella) mit Namen auf dem Cover zu zeigen. Die Antworten werden nach dem Sehen schriftlich festgehalten, ggf. mit einem Partner mithilfe eines Wörterbuches ergänzt und im gelenkten Unterrichtsgespräch verglichen.

Lösungsvorschlag zu *Copy 1*:

1. What kind of event is taking place? Where? And when?

It is a Christian procession; it is probably taking place in spring because of the flowers people are carrying (it is the Good Friday Parade), and it is in a town with typical English terraced houses. Everything is grey; the area looks poor.

2. Who is taking part? What are the people doing there?

White people, kids in uniform, priests in white garments, a music band playing drums and trumpets, Asian kids accompanied by a white English lady. They are marching in the street, carrying religious symbols such as a crucifix, wooden saints, and flowers.

3. What is the atmosphere like? How is this atmosphere created?

The atmosphere is one of joy, happiness and pleasure. This impression is conveyed by the rhythmic music and the words of the song such as "Glory, glory, glory, listen to the band, sing that same old story, ain't it something grand, to be as good as you can, like the banner man?"

Viewing comprehension: "Street parade"

1. What kind of event is taking place? Where? And when?

2. Who is taking part? What are the people doing there?

3. What is the atmosphere like? How is this atmosphere created?

4. What does Ella tell Annie and how does Ella look at this moment?

5. How do the children react to this message?

6. How does George look?

4. What does Ella tell Annie and how does she look at this moment?

"George is coming from the mosque." Ella looks worried.

5. How do the children react to this message?

They suddenly all run away from the parade straight into a nearby lane and into the parallel street. There they hide behind the houses when they see George standing at the corner. As soon as they feel safe, they pass behind him to join the parade at the next side alley. They are worried but not scared enough to leave the procession entirely.

6. How does George look?

He seems to feel satisfied because he is smiling. He greets Annie who has remained in the parade. He has no idea about his kids having taken part in the procession.

1.3 Sequence 2 – "Proud father"

Auch das nachfolgende Kapitel **(En: 3:02–9:26; Deu: 3:06–10:08)** dient mit den Aufgaben auf ***Copy 2*** einer Groborientierung, hier in Form einer Differenzierung zwischen den Charakteren und dem Erfassen der Filmhandlung. Die Schülerinnen und Schüler machen sich zunächst mit den Aufgaben bekannt. Ein einmaliges Sehen sollte zur nachfolgenden Bearbeitung der Aufgaben genügen.
Die Antworten zur Aufgabe 1 sollten gemeinsam besprochen werden, da viele Schüler noch Probleme haben werden, die Filmfiguren auseinanderzuhalten. Der Übersichtlichkeit halber sind im Lösungsvorschlag die Figuren an die richtige Stelle gesetzt worden. Die mit Pfeil im Lösungsvorschlag angegebenen Erläuterungen werden mündlich erarbeitet, um für den Subtext der sprachlichen Äußerungen zu sensibilisieren.
Mit Aufgabe 2 wird die offensichtlich gegen den Willen des Bräutigams arrangierte Heiratshandlung zusammengefasst. Diese Aufgabe ist einfach und kann von den Schülern in Partnerarbeit verglichen werden. Um Wortschatz zu üben, können sich die Schüler die Handlung noch einmal gegenseitig nacherzählen.
In Aufgabe 3, mit der der Filmausschnitt auch als Hausaufgabe (schriftlich) nachbearbeitet werden kann, werden erste Vermutungen über die Konfliktlage angestellt und es werden persönliche Eindrücke und Meinungen als innerer Monolog einer Filmfigur kreativ wiedergegeben. Eine vertiefte Behandlung des Themas „Heirat" bietet sich zu diesem frühen Stadium noch nicht an – sie erfolgt mit *Component 4*.

Lösungsvorschlag zu *Copy 2:*

1. Who says what? Try to identify the different characters and match them with the quotes. Then explain orally what the characters had in mind.

Ella, mother:	And take that bleeding parka off. → parka is not traditional Pakistani clothing
Mr Moorhouse:	Piccaninnies' fucking picnic. → hostility
George, father:	The watch. Here. Says your name in Arabic. Today you make me feel very proud. → watch as a symbol of the passing on of traditions; son is the father's pride and joy

Viewing comprehension: "Proud father"

1. Who says what? Try to identify the different characters and match them with the quotes. Then explain orally what the characters had in mind.

George, father	And take that bleeding parka off.
Ella, mother	Piccaninnies'[1] fucking picnic.
Nazir, eldest son	The watch. Here. Says your name in Arabic. Today you make me feel very proud.
Meenah, daughter	They just look funny, that's all.
Sajid, youngest son	I can't do this.
Mr Moorhouse, neighbour	I look stupid in this.
Stella Moorhouse, neighbour's granddaughter	I haven't got nits[2].

[1] **piccaninny** *(infml)* impolite word for a black child – [2] **nit** insect living in one's hair

2. Work out the correct order of the events in the marriage scene and write the appropriate numbers from 1 to 7 in the left-hand column.

	The parents are shocked. The bride looks worried. No-one knows how to interpret Nazir's reaction.
	Nazir parts his golden veil to have a look at the guests. He does not appear very happy but instead looks anxious.
	The silence is interrupted by the mullah's chant. The bride is unveiled. We see a beautiful girl who is as anxious as the bridegroom.
	The guests are sitting in a huge hall and waiting for the ceremony to start. Asian music is being played. The atmosphere is cheerful.
	Nazir's veil is lifted too. Both the bride and the bridegroom look at each other. There is silence.
	The music suddenly stops. The veiled bride is brought in. There are murmurings in the crowd. The bride is led up to the place beside the groom.
	Nazir rejects the golden ball. Staccato-type music starts. Nazir stands up, says he can't do it and escapes.

3. Do the following tasks. Then exchange your ideas.

a. Speculate about the match-making and the preparation of the marriage.
b. Why did Nazir reject this marriage against his father's will and all traditions?
c. What impact may Nazir's choice to flee have on the Khan family?
d. Prepare a short inner monologue of one of the characters in the scene: the bride, the bridegroom, the parents, one of the Khan siblings, the mullah, one of the guests. Then present your monologues.

Stella Moorhouse: They just look funny, that's all. → not hostile in contrast to her grandpa, is just interested

Nazir, eldest son: I can't do this. → cannot marry, motives not clear, at the very least it is not a marriage of love

Meenah, daughter: I look stupid in this. → does not like traditional Pakistani clothes

Sajid, youngest son: I haven't got nits. → a bit rebellious

2. Work out the correct order of the events in the marriage scene and write the appropriate numbers from 1 to 7 in the left-hand column.

7	The parents are shocked. The bride looks worried. No-one knows how to interpret Nazir's reaction.
2	Nazir parts his golden veil to have a look at the guests. He does not appear very happy but instead looks anxious.
4	The silence is interrupted by the mullah's chant. The bride is unveiled. We see a beautiful girl who is as anxious as the bridegroom.
1	The guests are sitting in a huge hall and waiting for the ceremony to start. Asian music is being played. The atmosphere is cheerful.
5	Nazir's veil is lifted too. Both the bride and the bridegroom look at each other. There is silence.
3	The music suddenly stops. The veiled bride is brought in. There are murmurings in the crowd. The bride is led up to the place beside the groom.
6	Nazir rejects the golden ball. Staccato-type music starts. Nazir stands up, says he can't do it and escapes.

Component 2

"East is East, and West is West, and never the twain shall meet" – Characters and conflicts

2.1 Vorbemerkung

Dieser Unterrichtsbaustein dient als Klammer für die im Verlaufe der gesamten Unterrichtseinheit von den Schülern selbstständig zu entwickelnde Charakterisierung der Filmfiguren und die Erarbeitung der Figurenkonstellation.
Die Schülerinnen und Schüler erhalten zunächst den Auftrag, sich über die Länge des Filmes auf eine Figur zu konzentrieren, um eine detaillierte Charakterisierung zu erarbeiten. Die Ergebnisse dieser *Long-term while-viewing task* können abschließend in einer schriftlichen Leistungsüberprüfung oder als Kurzreferat abgefragt werden. Sie können aber auch als Vorarbeit in das in *Component 4* vorgeschlagene Rollenspiel einer Talkshow (S. 73) eingehen, das zur Schulung mündlicher Fertigkeiten und ggf. als Leistungsüberprüfung eingesetzt werden kann.
Unter 2.4 sind Aufgaben zu finden, die sich nur auf die Sequenzen 3 bis 5 (Deu: Kapitel 3 und ein Teil von Kapitel 4) beziehen und auch ohne Berücksichtigung der in 2.2 und 2.3 vorgeschlagenen *Long-term while-viewing tasks* behandelt werden können, den Schülern aber überwiegend Beobachtungsaufträge anbieten, die ihnen helfen, eine Charakterisierung zu erarbeiten und die grundlegenden Konfliktlinien zu erfassen. Diese werden abschließend in einer Deutung des Filmtitels zusammengefasst.

2.2 A character map

Um die verschiedenen Filmfiguren namentlich identifizieren und in der Filmhandlung schnell wiedererkennen zu können, wird den Schülerinnen und Schülern mit der auf ***Copy 3*** abgedruckten *Character map* eine Orientierungshilfe an die Hand gegeben. Mithilfe der darauf abgebildeten Fotos sollen die Schüler sich zum einen eine Figur aussuchen, auf die sie sich konzentrieren (Aufgaben in Abschnitt 2.3).
Des Weiteren soll die hier unvollständig vorliegende *Character map* im Verlaufe der Unterrichtsstunden ausgefüllt werden. Dazu muss erläutert werden, wie eine solche Übersicht entwickelt wird und welche Funktion sie hat. Eine Beispiellösung ist auf Seite 38 abgedruckt.

Was ist eine *Character map* und wie wird sie entwickelt?

Die Charaktere einer Geschichte werden mit ihren hervorstechendsten Eigenschaften bezeichnet und durch Pfeile zueinander in Beziehung gesetzt, auf denen wiederum die markanteste Handlung bzw. Einstellung zu den jeweils anderen Charakteren festgehalten wird. Verschiedene Gruppierungen kann man zudem farblich kennzeichnen, um z. B. Gegensätze und Konflikte herauszuarbeiten. Bei vorliegendem Beispiel können verschiedene Farben für

Character map

Poppah Khalid

George Khan

Ella Khan

Annie

arranges his marriage

disappoints him by fleeing from marriage

Nazir Khan,
shy, frightened …

Abdul Khan

Tariq Khan

Maneer Khan

Saleem Khan

Meenah Khan

Sajid Khan

Stella Moorhouse

Earnest Moorhouse

Character map

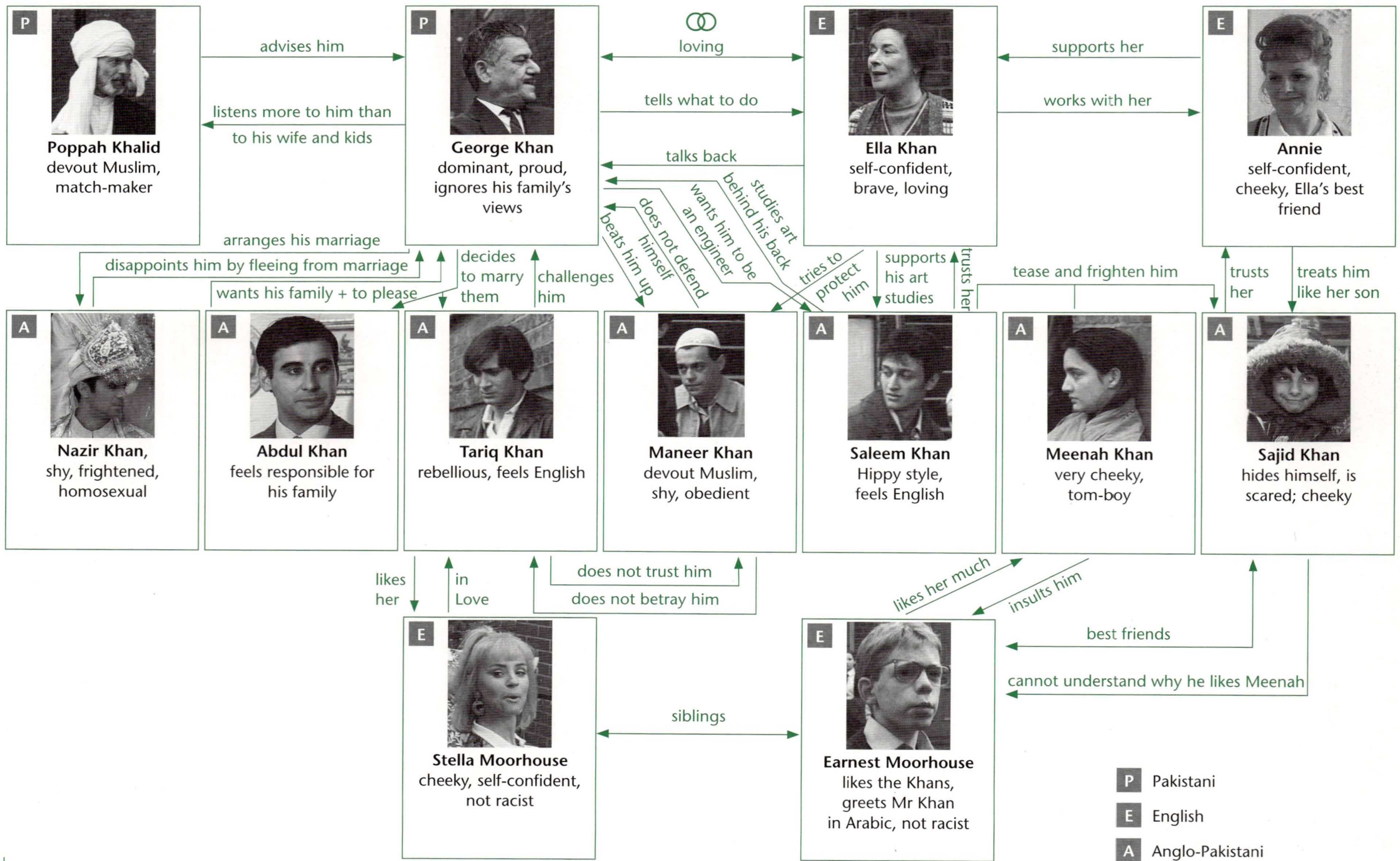

die Zugehörigkeit zu den unterschiedlichen Nationalitäten und Kulturen verwendet werden. Es entsteht so eine visualisierte Handlungsstruktur und Figurenkonstellation, die hilft, die wesentlichen Elemente einer Geschichte und deren absichtsvolle Konstruiertheit zu erfassen. Eine *Character map* eignet sich auch hervorragend als Merkzettel zum Nacherzählen einer Geschichte oder eines Films. Mit der Methode der *Character map* können Schüler und Schülerinnen zudem selbst Geschichten bzw. *Story boards* entwickeln.

2.3 Long-term while-viewing task: Characterization

Die Schülerinnen und Schüler suchen sich eine Figur aus, über die sie auf ***Copy 4***, einem *Character sheet,* Beobachtungen stichpunktartig festhalten. Es sollte abgesichert werden, dass möglichst alle relevanten Figuren auf die Schüler verteilt werden.
Die Ergebnisse können dann im Rahmen der Behandlung von *Component 4* vor dem *Role play* verglichen werden (wird das *Role play* nicht gemacht, können die Ergebnisse auch nach dem Ende des Films verglichen werden). Der Vergleich kann in Form von Einzelreferaten erfolgen oder als Gruppenpräsentation, nachdem die Schüler, die sich für dieselben Filmfiguren entschieden haben, zuvor ihre Ergebnisse zusammengetragen und ergänzt haben.

Lösungsvorschlag zu *Copy 4*: Sajid Khan (Beispiel)

1. What is the character's **position in society** in general and her or his community and/or family more specifically?
   - youngest son, Ella's baby, is always made fun of and teased by his siblings
   - his best friend is Earnest, a white, red-haired English boy from the neighbourhood; Sajid is accepted by the white kids in the street

2. What is her or his **outward appearance** (clothes, haircut)? What does this choice of appearance **mean**?
   - has got quite long dark hair and a childish face
   - always wears a hooded parka and refuses to wear traditional Pakistani clothes; the parka is like a protection for him

3. How does the character **feel**? Towards which people? When?
   - is frightened of his father, hides from him
   - looks to his mother, Auntie Annie and Abdul for protection
   - is curious about sexual things, spies on his brother, feels annoyed by his siblings, except for Maneer and Abdul
   - is quite cheeky and rebellious with the Shah family: the Pakis

4. What are the character's **attitudes** and **behaviour** and what are the **motives** behind these?
   - does not want to go to the mosque → hides → is not interested in religious education, feels more English
   - does not want to be circumcised → hides → is frightened
   - often feels annoyed by his siblings → hides
   - does not want to take off his parka → hides → protection
   - calls the Shahs "the Pakis"→ feels English himself

Long-term while-viewing task: Character sheet

Choose one character of the movie: ______________________________.
While watching the movie, focus on your character and take notes on the following questions.

1. What is the character's **position in society in general** and her or his community and/or family more specifically?

____

____

____

2. What is her or his **outward appearance** (clothes, haircut)? What does this choice of appearance **mean**?

____

____

____

3. How does the character **feel**? Towards which people? When?

____

____

____

4. What are the character's **attitudes** and **behaviour** and what are the **motives** behind these?

____

____

____

____

5. What is the character's **relationship** to other characters?

____

____

____

6. Is there any **development** of the character? What development(s)? **Why?**

____

____

7. Is it a main ☐ an intermediate ☐ a background character? ☐
Is it a more static (remains stable) ☐☐☐☐☐ or more dynamic character? (changes)
Is it a flat (single quality) ☐☐☐☐☐ or a more complex individual?

5. What is the character's **relationship** to other characters?

- feels affection towards Nazir and Abdul, his eldest brothers
- feels annoyed by the other brothers and his sister
- likes Auntie Annie, loves his mother, accepts his father
- has got white English friends in the street

6. Is there any **development** of the character? What development(s)? Why?

- takes off his parka at the end → liberation, does not have to protect himself anymore

Abhängig von der eigenen Wahrnehmung der Filmfigur müssten dann noch die *Copy 4* abschließenden Fragen zur Figur beantwortet und begründet werden.
Als Hausaufgabe könnten die Notizen zur Charakterisierung einer Figur als Text ausformuliert werden. Eine schriftliche Leistungsüberprüfung ist alternativ denkbar. Eine kurze Übersicht als Vergleichsgrundlage ist unter *Plot and characters* (S. 6 ff.) abgedruckt. Eine ganze Reihe von Beispieltexten ist unter Schoolmaster_Wiki, der freien Wissensdatenbank für Schüler, zu finden: www.wiki.klemm-site.de/wiki/index.php.

Drei Beispiele für Schülerarbeiten:

Meenah Khan – played by Archie Panjabi – is the only girl of the Khan children. Meenah is a very cheeky girl and she doesn't feel like a Pakistani. She is educated at an English school and she wants to be like all the other girls there. On the one hand, she behaves like a normal girl that stands under the pressure of her father. She answers back when George puts his foot down and when she is left alone she behaves crazy. On the other hand, she is a very special girl, because she likes to play football and does other "masculine" activities. Maybe, this is the reason why her little brother's friend Earnest has fallen in love with her.
Concerning her family, she is on the side of her mother and her brothers. Therefore, she goes with her brothers when they decide to break away from home. That's why she has got a very good and warm relationship to her brothers, except for the youngest one. All she has to do with Sajid is to banter and to needle him. I think she has a special relationship with her mother. As the only girl in the family, her mother grants her a special status, although her mother gets angry, when Meenah talks badly about her father.
During the film, Meenah's character is changing in some ways. At the beginning of the film, she fights against her father all the time, never minding whether there is a reason or not, but at the end of the film she learns to sometimes shut up and to think about what to say. All in all, you can say that Meenah is an interesting character and that it was a great pleasure to follow her development.

(by Caroline, www.wiki.klemm-site.de/wiki/index.php/Meenah)

Abdul (Raji James) is one of the elder sons of Ella and George. Abdul is the hardworking son whose character remains ambiguous until the end of the film because the audience never knows what he really thinks. However, in my opinion Abdul actually feels as British as all the other children. At the beginning of the movie, the audience is given only a

little information about Abdul since he stays in the background more quietly. I would suppose that he is the kind of son who does not cause any trouble. This becomes obvious when you watch his behaviour towards his father because he does not let him know that actually, more or less, he is against Pakistani traditions. Abdul's father arranges the marriage between Abdul and an ugly Pakistani girl. Though Abdul is against this marriage, he would do it just to please his father because he seems to have too much respect to show him his true feelings.
The development of Abdul is discernible when George Khan wants to beat Ella, Abdul's mother. It is then that he shows courage. He protects his mother by preventing the violence of the father. In this scene, which takes place in the last part of the movie, Abdul's character seems to become stronger and he recognizes that someone must show George a limit, because it goes too far if George is ready to beat his wife.
In general, I would say that Abdul is a strong character but he is not a very marked one because he is one of the most well-behaved and quiet sons.

(www.wiki.klemm-site.de/wiki/index.php/Abdul)

Stella Moorhouse – played by Emma Rydal – is a blonde, pretty, sometimes naive teenage girl, who lives with her brother Earnest and with her grandfather in the neighbourhood of the Khan family. Her grandfather is the only person who cannot bear that a Pakistani family lives next to him. But Stella does not care about it and is happily in love with one of the Khans' boys, Tariq. Both spend much of their time sneaking kisses in the alley behind their homes. But it seems as if Stella was the only one in the relationship who has really deep feelings.
When Sajid tells Tariq that their father has promised Tariq and one of his brothers to two Pakistani girls, Tariq leaves home with his siblings and Stella is willing to come with him but Tariq doesn't care about her. For him the "relationship" is more like a game. If Stella is not around, he flirts with other girls and even if she finds out, he does not care about her feelings.
At the end of the movie, it seems that Stella has realized what kind of guy Tariq is and what kind of relationship they had, but I also think that she will go back to him any time he asks her to.

(by Johanna, www.wiki.klemm-site.de/wiki/index.php/Stella)

2.4 Sequences 3 to 5 with film title

Die Filmsequenzen 3 bis 5 **(En: 9:27–27:07; Deu, Kapitel 3 und ein Teil von 4: 10:09–27:49)** werden zweimal (ggf. in zwei Unterrichtsstunden) – möglichst mit englischen Untertiteln – gesehen. Die Aufgaben sind a) auf globales und b) auf detailliertes Verständnis ausgerichtet.

Die folgenden **globalen Beobachtungsaufträge** sollen helfen, ein allgemeines Verständnis abzusichern und sich Informationen für die *Character map* und das *Character sheet* zu erschließen.

(Concentrate on the character you have chosen and) find out
- about the relationship of the members of the Khan family and the English neighbours
- about the importance of religion and culture for George
- about the Khan kids' attitude to religion and being taught about Islam
- about the relationship between Ella and George, their children

→ **How are the Khans torn between two cultures?**

Das dynamisch im Unterrichtsgespräch zu entwickelnde Tafelbild dient als Sammlung von Zwischenergebnissen nach diesem ersten Sehvorgang.

"East is East, and West is West, …"

↙ ↘ ↙ ↘

Pakistani culture & Muslim religion	**← the Khans →**	**English people & culture**
thinks he should have moved to Bradford	George	greets the priest, but thinks he is stupid; both are friendly
listens to the news about Pakistan		seems to like Annie
insists on his children being taught about Islam		accepts Ella refusing to let his Pakistani family come over
insists on Sajid's circumcision = his religion		
is against George's second wife coming to England	Ella	in the chip shop with Annie: serves English customers
accepts that all boys have to be circumcised		talks to the priest and gives him flowers behind George's back
hides from going to the mosque	Sajid	plays with Earnest Moorhouse
dances to Asian music	Meenah	plays football with English kids
reluctantly go to the mosque, no idea of Arabic, not interested in Quran	Tariq	sneaks kisses with Stella Moorhouse
	Saleem	studies art
		the latter three eat bacon, watch an English politician's speech about repatriation
is a devout Muslim	Maneer	
does not drink, so does not take part in the stag party of his workmates	Abdul	works with male English colleagues

"… and never the twain shall meet"?

Abschließend erfolgt die Ergänzung des in der Überschrift begonnenen Titelzitats, über dessen Bedeutung und Richtigkeit nun spekuliert wird.

The title of the film "East is East" is taken from a ballad by Rudyard Kipling. The ballad goes on with "... and never the twain shall meet." What could this line mean against the background of what we have just found out about the Khan family?

Is it true that East and West will never meet? Justify with examples from the film and your ideas on how the film will go on.

Die Schülerinnen und Schüler haben mit dieser Aufgabenstellung Gelegenheit, das Tafelbild noch einmal insgesamt in seinem Aussagegehalt zum Filmbeginn zu überdenken und zu überlegen, wie die Handlung weiterverlaufen wird.
Daraufhin wird Kiplings Balladenbeginn, den die Schüler als Tafelanschrieb oder Kopie erhalten, in Beziehung zum Filmtitel gesetzt. Dies kann als Hausaufgabe (ggf. mit Internetrecherche zur Ballade und zu Kipling) erteilt werden.
Sollten die Aufgaben zur Charakterisierung aus 2.2 und 2.3 nicht erteilt worden sein (dann geklammerten Aufgabenteil auf Seite 43 „Concentrate ..." weglassen), können alternativ das Zitat und ein *intelligent guessing about its meaning* als Einstieg in die Unterrichtseinheit und der Balladenbeginn als Abschluss dienen.

Read the poem by Rudyard Kipling.
What is the speaker's idea about East and West?
How do you interpret the poem with regard to the first chapters of the film?

Rudyard Kipling: The Ballad of East and West

Oh, East is East, and West is West, and never the twain shall meet,
Till Earth and Sky stand presently at God's great Judgement Seat;
But there is neither East nor West, Border, nor Breed, nor Birth,
When two strong men stand face to face,
Though they come from the ends of the earth! (1889)

Der Satz „East is East, and West is West" gehört nicht nur zu den bekanntesten, sondern auch zu den am meisten falsch zitierten und interpretierten Sprachschöpfungen von Rudyard Kipling. Eine Interpretation des Balladenanfangs in Bezug auf den Film kann daher nur subjektiv und losgelöst vom Originalkontext sein. Die Ballade selbst hat folgenden Inhalt:

It is the story of Kamal, a Pashtun (= Indian tribe) brigand, who sneaked over the border and stole the horse of a British colonel who was head of a detachment of Raj Guides (Raj = rule of the British government in India). The colonel's son chased Kamal and caught up with him. The two then realized that they were both brave men, so Kamal sent his own son to escort the colonel's son back to the guides' camp. Nevertheless, Kamal's son then abandoned his work as a brigand and became a Raj Guide, too. These rides were dangerous because behind every rock there was a Kamal man hiding with a gun.

Lösungsvorschlag:

What is the speaker's idea about East and West?

The speaker's idea about East and West is first that the two (= twain) are so different that they could never coexist together on Earth. This will remain the case until the two meet in heaven where everyone is equal before God. In heaven, there is no border, no difference of birth or race, no East or West. However, when two strong men who are both courageous face each other, then there is no difference either, even if they come from the two ends of the earth. Thus, in the end, it is the character of a person that is more important than one's origins.

How do you interpret the poem with regard to the first chapters of the film?

East and West, Pakistani and British culture seem to contradict each other. This view is represented most clearly by George. However, it is up to the people involved to reconcile the two cultures. That this may be possible is demonstrated most clearly by the Khan kids, who have fewer problems than their father living in their English environment. Nevertheless, they also try to avoid parts of their Pakistani culture, which seems to be the reason for the family conflicts as can already be seen with Nazir's marriage.

Es ist zu erwarten, dass die Schüler nach dem ersten Sehen spezifische kulturelle und religiöse Besonderheiten wie die Beschneidung und Georges Status als Immigrant mit einer weiteren Familie in Pakistan wie auch sprachliche Besonderheiten wenig erfasst und genau verstanden haben (zumal sie sich ggf. ja auch auf „ihre Charaktere" konzentrieren sollten).

Ein zweiter Sehvorgang zielt daher mit den Aufgaben auf ***Copy 5*** auf ein **detaillierteres Verstehen**. Die Aufgaben werden vor dem Sehen durchgelesen und ggf. besprochen. Die Schüler benutzen für Aufgabe 2b verschiedene Farben für Ella (rot) und George (blau), um deren Einstellung gegenüber Pakistan und Georges Familie mit passenden Adjektiven kenntlich zu machen. Der Film kann ggf. nach der Szene im *Chip shop* und Georges und Ellas Dialog kurz angehalten werden, damit Aufgabe 2a besser bearbeitet werden kann. Nach dem Sehen werden die Ergebnisse für die Aufgaben 1, 2c und 3 gemeinsam besprochen. Aufgaben 2a und b können in Partnerarbeit verglichen werden. Alternativ können die Aufgaben 2 und 3 vor dem Sehen auf zwei Gruppen aufgeteilt werden, die ihre Ergebnisse dann in Partnerarbeit austauschen.

Viewing comprehension and analysis: Sequences 3 to 5

1. Sequences 3 and 5: Poppah Khalid and George

Explain the meaning of the following statements:

a. "It will always be difficult for you, Zaheed. They are different."

b. "Until your sons join the community fully, they will always be a worry for you."

2. Sequences 3 and 4: George and Ella

a. Complete the following dialogue with the words given.

border – read – foot – Indians – problem – worry – government – wife – rebels – talk – treat – danger – hand – darling

RADIO: The Islamabad ______________ has also accused India of supplying arms to ______________ in East Pakistan.
GEORGE: These bastard ______________. No bloody interest in East Pakistan. Only want Azaad Kashmir. I bloody ______________ Family live on ______________ they may be in______________.
ELLA: The answer's no.
GEORGE: What you bloody talking about, 'No'. I no bloody ask you anything.
ELLA: I can ______________ your mind like the back of me ______________, so you can piss off if you think you're bringing her over here.
GEORGE: Why you ______________ to me like this, my ______________?
ELLA: If she sets ______________ in this country, I'm off and I'll take the bloody kids with me.
GEORGE: Why big ______________? First ______________ always ______________ second like sister.
ELLA: Get stuffed! ... Who's next? (to customers)

b. What is George's and Ella's attitude to Pakistan and George's family there? Use different colours to underline appropriate adjectives. Justify your choice orally.

angry – adamant – aggressive – furious – cheeky – fearless – innocent – interested – jealous – intimidated – loving – provoking – rebellious – shy – suspicious – threatening

c. Describe the still. What does Ella want to show and why?

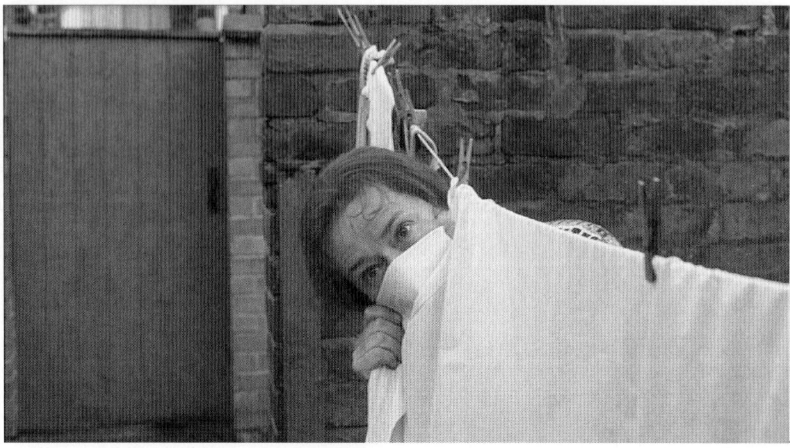

3. Sequence 4: 'Circumcision' – a language taboo?

a. Sajid has not yet been circumcised. He has to undergo the operation. What is circumcision?

b. Different words are used by the film characters to talk about the topic 'circumcision'. The vocabulary and the grammar of sentences used in a certain situation can be described with the term 'register'. Put in the following words either to 'formal' or 'informal' register into the inner circle of the wheel:

foreskin – knob – penis – tickle-tackle – They were all done. – We fixes. – The circumcision was absolutely fine. – This thing has to be cutting.

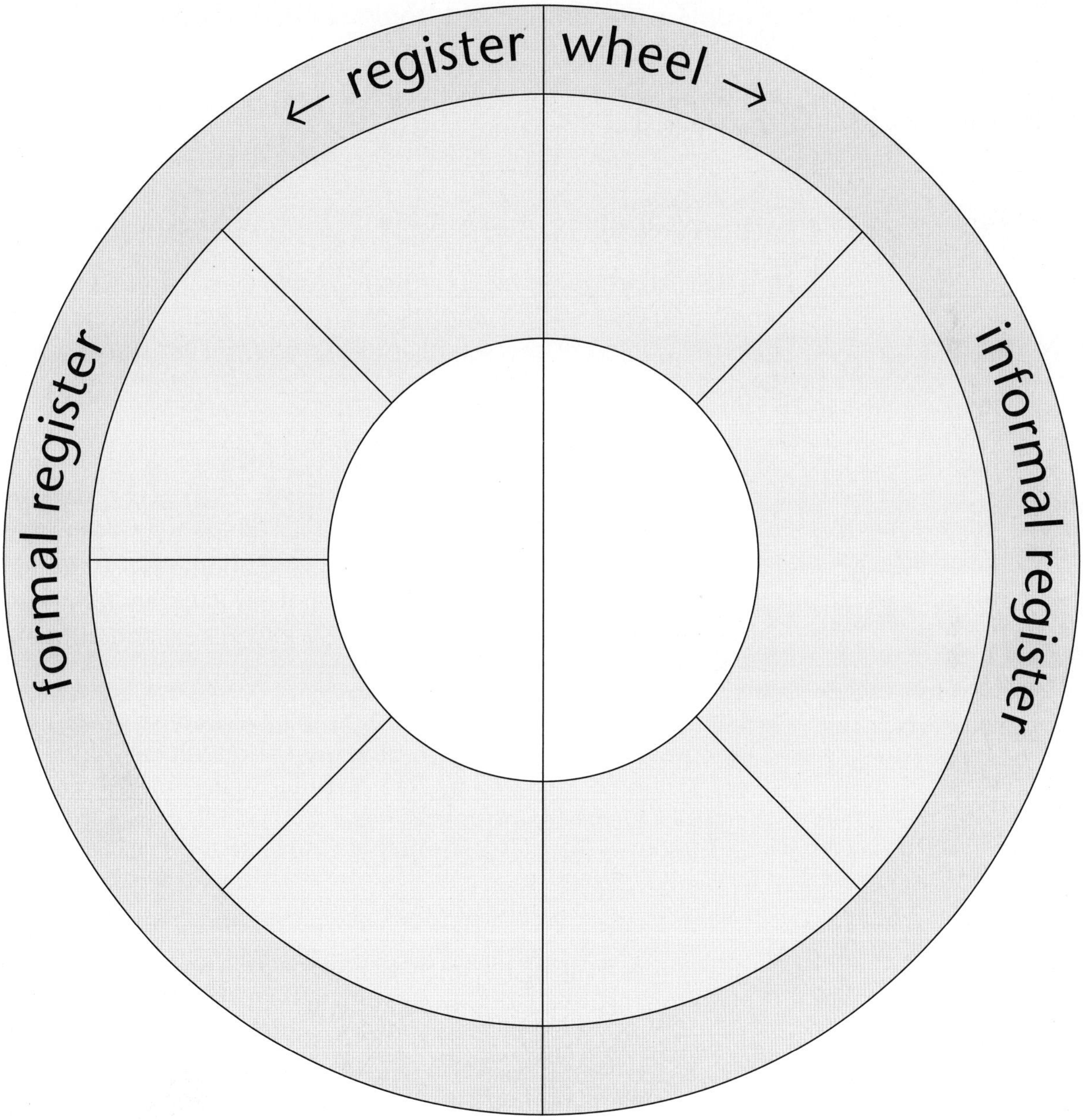

c. Then write the names of the characters who use the words and phrases into the outer circle. Add the reasons for their use of informal or formal register.

d. Why did Ella accept having Sajid circumcised?

Lösungsvorschlag zu *Copy 5*:

1. Poppah Khalid and George
   Explain the meaning of the following statements:
   a. "It will always be difficult for you, Zaheed. They are different."

   Even if George had moved to Bradford, it would not have changed his situation to any great degree. Through being married to an English woman, his family is necessarily more strongly influenced by an English environment. His kids are therefore different from Pakistani kids.

   b. "Until your sons join the community fully, they will always be a worry for you."

   By this, he means that George's sons should marry a Pakistani woman and not an English one.

2. George and Ella
   a. Complete the following dialogue with the words given.

   the Islamabad *government;* arms to *rebels;* bastard *Indians;* I bloody *worry;* on *border;* be in *danger,* I can *read;* back of me *hand;* Why you *talk;* my *darling;* If she sets *foot;* big *problem;* First *wife* always *treat* second

   b. What is George's and Ella's attitude to Pakistan and George's family there?

   George: gets angry about the news, seems to be interested in Pakistan; is cheeky with Ella when talking about his first wife; at first plays the innocent when talking about his Pakistani family as if he did not know about Ella's opinion; is a loving husband but provokes Ella with his suggestions

   Ella: is adamant about not wanting to have George's Pakistani family come over to England; is obviously also a bit jealous of the first wife; is not intimidated by George but instead rebellious and suspicious of him listening to the news and talking about the situation in Pakistan as she is not interested in the news.

   c. Describe the still. What does Ella want to show and why?

   Ellas hides half of her face behind a bedsheet. She is mocking George's first wife who must remain veiled in Pakistan. Ella points out that George's first wife would not be able nor willing to work as hard as she does in the chip shop to earn a living. In this way, Ella refutes George's idea of bringing his Pakistani wife over to England.

3. 'Circumcision' – a language taboo?
   a. What is circumcision?

   The foreskin of the penis is removed. This is practiced by Muslims for religious reasons, and for reasons of hygiene.

b. and c. The register wheel

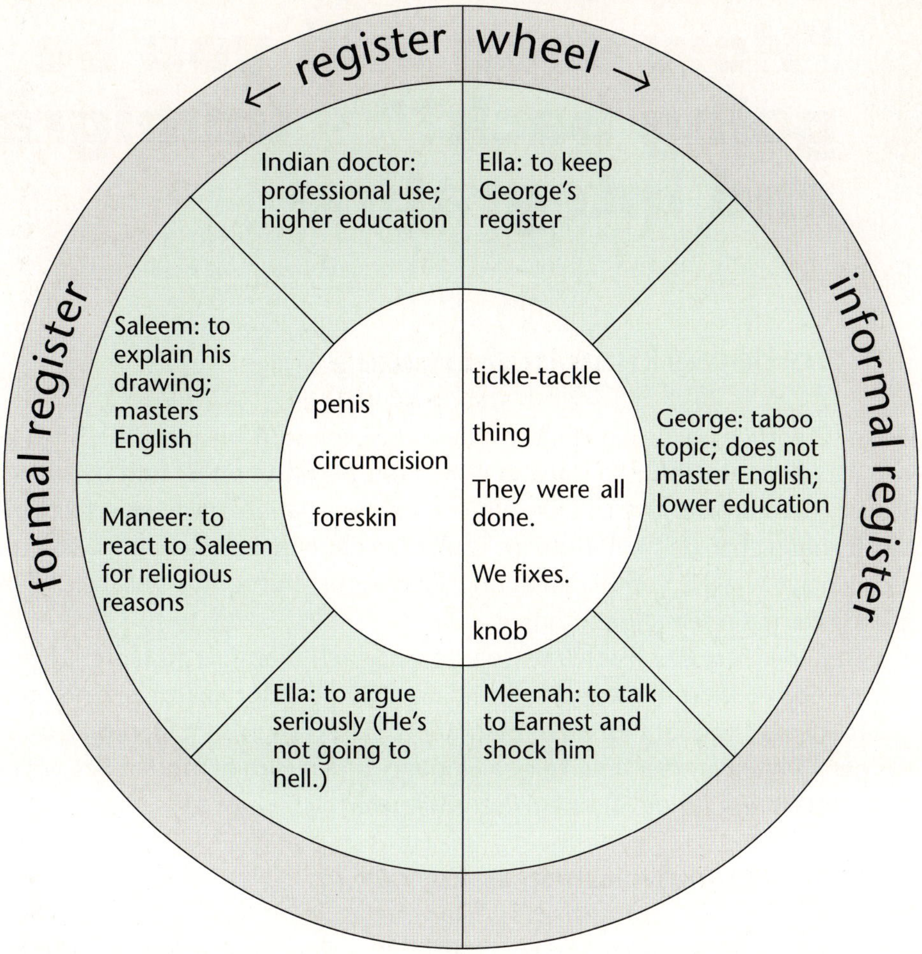

d. Why did Ella accept having Sajid circumcised?

When Ella married George, she knew that she would have to accept Islam and follow at least some of its rules such as circumcision. For George, his religion is a source of identity. For this reason, if his wife were to contradict him and refuse an important religious practice such as circumcision, he would feel attacked. To keep the peace and protect her marriage, Ella had to agree to the practice.

Als Hausaufgabe erhalten die Schüler den Auftrag, die Inhalte der Kapitel 3 bis 5 in ihr *Character sheet* und die *Character map* einzuarbeiten.
Alternativ wäre denkbar, das *Register wheel* aus Aufgabe 3 als Text zu versprachlichen und die Verwendung des jeweiligen Registers durch einzelne Figuren im situativen Kontext zu begründen. Aufgabenstellung:

How do the different characters in the film (George, Ella, Meenah, Tariq, Saleem, Maneer, Earnest, the doctor, Annie) react to the fact that Sajid has to be circumcised?

Component 3

"How soon will you be going back?" – Immigration and integration

3.1 Vorbemerkung und Einstieg

Dieser Unterrichtsbaustein stellt mit den **Sequenzen 6 bis einschließlich des ersten Teils von 10 (Deu: ein Teil von Kapitel 4 bis zum Beginn von 8**) und dem hier stattfindenden Besuch der Familie Khan in Bradford die Immigration pakistanischer Einwanderer nach Großbritannien in den Mittelpunkt. Es werden daher neben den Aufgaben zum Film – hauptsächlich zur Analyse von Bildausschnitt und Kameraführung – zusätzliche Texte mit Hintergrundinformationen angeboten.
Am Ende der Sequenz 5 schlägt George vor, nach Bradford zu fahren. Hierauf bezieht sich der auf ***Copy 6*** konzipierte (als Folie auf dem Overheadprojektor zu präsentierende) Einstieg in das Thema „Immigration und Integration". Die Fragen zum Standbild und zum Ausschnitt aus dem *Screenplay,* der aber keinen Eingang in den Film gefunden hat, sollen die Schülerinnen und Schüler für die Thematik sensibilisieren.

Lösungsvorschlag zu *Copy 6:*

1. The town sign for Bradford, a town in the north of England, has been changed. Speculate about the reasons for this.

   As George wants to go to see his family in Bradford, it can be supposed that Bradistan, the name written in graffiti over the real town sign, has been coined from a blend of Bradford and Pakistan. Probably, a majority of people from Pakistan live in Bradford to keep their community alive in England.

2. Read out the dialogue from the screenplay in roles. Explain how the Khan kids see their identity.

   The dialogue reveals that the Khan kids do not have a clear or uniform view of their identity, although everyone has his or her own idea of it.
   Saleem refers to his English mother and his Asian father when he says he is Anglo-Indian. However, this would only be partly correct since his father sees himself as a Pakistani and many Muslim Indians left India for Pakistan in the course of the war for independence in India. One can therefore suppose that George or his family must have at some stage emigrated from India to the newly-founded nation of Pakistan. Another possibility is that Saleem does not differentiate between Indian and Pakistani origins.
   Meenah enthusiastically calls herself Eurasian to avoid any national references but Saleem reveals this idea to be a euphemism.

"Being Pakistani is more than Bradford"

SALEEM: I thought we were Anglo-Indian.

MEENAH: We're Eurasian.

SALEEM: Sounds more romantic than Paki, I suppose.

TARIQ: We're English.

MANEER: We're not! No one round here thinks we're English. We're the Pakis who run the chippy.

TARIQ: If you want to be Pakistani why don't you fuck off to Bradford and take me dad with you.

MANEER: Being Pakistani is more than Bradford, Tariq.

Ayub Din-Khan: East is East. A Screenplay. Royal Court Theatre, 1996

1. The town sign for Bradford, a town in the north of England, has been changed. Speculate about the reasons for this.
2. Read out the dialogue from the screenplay in roles. Explain how the Khan kids see their identity.

Tariq is adamant that they are English. He denies his Pakistani origins. This is also expressed in his reproach to Maneer about moving to Bradford.
Maneer is more realistic. He knows that the English in Salford do not see the Khan family as being English but instead as 'the Pakis' who do cheap work and do not have a good reputation. Nevertheless, he also knows that moving to Bradford would not be sufficient to gain acceptance as Pakistani.

3.2 Sequences 6 and 7 – Bradford

Zum nächsten Aspekt wird mit der Frage übergeleitet, ob die Kinder sich wohl in Bradford besser aufgehoben fühlen werden und ob ihnen die *Bradford community* helfen wird, eine Identität zu finden. Was macht Bradford aus? Und warum will George dort hinfahren?
Vor dem einmaligen Sehen von Sequenz 6 **(En: 27:08–35:29; Deu, Kapitel 4 ab: 27:16 bis zum Ende: 35:39)** machen die Schülerinnen und Schüler sich mit Aufgabe 1 auf ***Copy 7*** vertraut, die im Anschluss an das Sehen in Partnerarbeit verglichen wird. Aufgabe 2 wird gemeinsam besprochen. Es wird für 2b vorausgesetzt, dass den Schülern bereits die Terminologie der Filmmittel bekannt ist bzw. entsprechende Informationen zum Nachschlagen bereitstehen.

Lösungsvorschlag zu *Copy 7*, Aufgaben 1 und 2:

1. a. Right or wrong? Correct the wrong statements.

1. It was not Maneer but Abdul.
3. He just played an Indian who shouted to "kill bloody English" in a film.
6. Ella knows that George says it because he would like to move there but she makes it clear that she refuses to do so.
7. Except George's boys.
8. No, they are in another room and are talking about the daughter of Ella's English friend.

b. Why does George agree with the proposals for his sons?

Obviously, he also finds Mr Shah's daughters not particularly attractive but he does not want to lose face. In addition, Mr Shah seems to be a wealthy man so that would make it a good match.

2. Have a close look at the two stills from the sequence.
a. What do they show about the status of women and men in the Pakistani community? Why is Ella's friend weeping?

Men hold council on important decisions such as match-making. Women are excluded. It is thus a highly patriarchal society where men dominate and women have to obey. The daughter of Ella's English friend is married in Pakistan.

b. Decide between the given terms for field size and camera angle and mark them in two colours according to the stills. What is the effect on the viewer?

Still 'English women': The field size is a medium shot to show the two women's close relationship. It is a neutral eye-level shot. Both women feel the same – very sad. Staying in the kitchen symbolizes their expected role.
Still 'Bradford men': The field size is a long shot and the camera angle is an establishing shot to show the beginning scene as a whole from a certain perspective. The council seems to be serious.

Bleibt nicht ausreichend Unterrichtszeit, um die nachfolgende Sequenz mit Aufgabe 3a zu beenden, so könnte man hier zum Beispiel die Aufgabe erteilen, die gesehenen Szenen (improvisierend) nachzuspielen und ggf. um eigene Ideen zu erweitern bzw. dies als Hausaufgabe vorzubereiten. Mögliche Aufgabenstellungen dazu:

- Imagine you are Saleem, Tariq, Abdul, Maneer and Sajid. You have just left the group of Pakistani men with your father and now exchange your impressions outside.
- You belong to the group of Pakistani men in Bradford and want to know from George how he manages life in Salford and whether he has problems with his kids.
- You are Meenah and you want to know about the daughter of your mother's friend who is married in Pakistan.
- Ella and her English friend talk about their daughters and how their respective fates are determined by their fathers.

In der Sequenz 7 **(En: 35:30–41:57; Deu, Kapitel 5 und ein Teil von 6: 35:40–42:06)** erleben die Khan-Kinder, insbesondere die angehenden Bräutigame Abdul und Tariq, geradezu kontrastiv das Leben in Bradford und in Salford. Mithilfe der Standbilder auf ***Copy 7***, Aufgabe 3 kann über die Unterschiede zwischen den zwei Kulturen spekulierend auf die Sequenz eingestimmt werden bzw. die jeweils ersten beiden Standbilder werden analysiert, da sie vom Beginn der Sequenz 6 sind.

Die Schüler lesen sich dann Aufgabe 3a durch und entscheiden sich in Partnerarbeit für die Konzentration auf Bradford und die pakistanische Gemeinde oder auf Salford und die englische Gemeinde. Sie machen sich nach einem einmaligen Sehen Notizen, die sie dann austauschen.

Viewing comprehension and analysis: Sequences 6 and 7

1. Watch sequence 6: "Your daughters are my daughters"

a. Tick right or wrong. Correct the wrong statements orally.

No.	Statement	Right	Wrong
1	George secretly takes the photos of Tariq and Maneer.		
2	On their way to Bradford Asian music is playing as the soundtrack.		
3	When George came to England he was a shouting star in a film.		
4	George did not have any luggage then. Now he has got his own business.		
5	Bradford is like a big oriental market. Many people wear traditional clothes.		
6	George says that all are happy and Ella absolutely agrees with him.		
7	All men in the house wear a traditional Jinnah hat. All can speak Urdu.		
8	Ella and an English woman, also married to a Pakistani, do shopping.		
9	George tells Mr Shah that one of his sons is dead.		
10	All agree that Mr Shah's daughters are beautiful.		

b. Why does George agree with the proposals for his sons?

____

2. Have a close look at the two stills from the sequence.

a. What do they show about the status of women and men in the Pakistani community? Why is Ella's friend weeping?

____

____

____

b. Decide between the given terms for field size and camera angle and mark them in two colours according to the stills. What is the effect on the viewer?

close-up – medium shot – long shot – high-angle shot – eye-level shot – establishing shot

Effect: ______________________________

3. Watch sequence 7: "A night on the town"

a. How do the Khan kids experience Pakistani life in Bradford and English life in Salford? Organize your information in a table. Use the stills given to illustrate your findings.

b. Analyse field size and camera work of the stills. How does the director create the contrast between Pakistani and English life?

c. Explain why "Being Pakistani is more than Bradford".

Brad~~ford~~istan	**Salford**
 Arriving in Bradford	 Leaving Salford
 At the cinema	 At the entrance of the disco
 A Bollywood romance	 English courting

Ggf. wird die Grundstruktur für die unten stehende Tabelle zuvor vorgegeben (gemeinsam erarbeitet). Eine Gruppe könnte dann ihre Erkenntnisse für alle vortragen, welche als Tafelbild festgehalten bzw. ergänzt werden.

	Pakistani life in Bradford	**English life in Salford**
In the street	• many people in the streets, very lively and busy • a street market with many stalls: spices, food, etc. • all very colourful	• no people in the streets, empty, seemingly dead • depressing, dark colours of houses and the street
Atmosphere	• exotic, inviting, cheerful	• depressing, sad
People	• in traditional colourful clothes; some in western clothes but only men • everything is done for one's family, even the film is changed	• some young English people are hostile to foreign-looking people → immigrants: not allowed to go into the disco, for "members only"
Courting	• a Bollywood romance shows a couple who has fallen in love • Ella and George feel reminded of their past and hug each other • Abdul and Tariq like the film with its model of romantic love	• young people meet outside, even girls • they smoke, drink, dance, flirt, kiss • there is not much romance, just jealousy and advances

Für die Bearbeitung der Aufgabe 3b kann die Tabelle auf ***Copy 8*** zur Verfügung gestellt werden. Diese Aufgabe können die Schüler selbstständig oder in Partnerarbeit erledigen oder – da mindestens 30 Minuten eingeplant werden müssen – sie wird als Hausaufgabe aufgegeben. Der Vergleich sollte gemeinsam erfolgen, insbesondere wenn eine Leistungsüberprüfung vorgesehen ist, die eine Analyse von Filmtechniken beinhalten soll. Die Ergebnisse von Aufgabe 3b (s. S. 58) sind Voraussetzung für 3c. Die von Maneer geäußerte Vermutung, dass Bradford noch lange keinen wahren Pakistani macht (vgl. *Copy 6*, S. 51), soll nun unter Bezug auf die Filmszenen erläutert werden.

Lösungsvorschlag zu *Copy 7*, Aufgabe 3c:

Explain why "Being Pakistani is more than Bradford".

George thinks that it would be easier for him to keep his Pakistani traditions alive and educate his children in this way if he lived in Bradford. What he seems to deny is that not only did he move outside his community but he also decided to marry an English woman. As Ella is absolutely unwilling to live completely like a Muslim wife, even if she often makes compromises, the kids would always be influenced by the other culture, even more so because they live in England. Being Pakistani means being a devout Muslim like Maneer. It also means accepting the rules of Islam such as not eating pork or smoking. It does not mean hiding in a cultural enclave like Bradford. In reality, it may be true that one can only be a proper Pakistani in one's own country, in Pakistan.

Worksheet – "A night on the town": Analysis of field size and camera work of stills

Still	Field size	Camera angle	Camera position	Camera movement	How does the director create the contrast between Pakistani and English life?
Arriving in Bradford					
Leaving Salford					
At the cinema					
At the entrance of the disco					
A Bollywood romance					
English courting					

Model answer – "A night on the town": Analysis of field size and camera work of stills

Still	Field size	Camera angle	Camera position	Camera movement	How does the director create the contrast between Pakistani and English life?
Arriving in Bradford	medium shot to see the market in the street	eye-level shot to show neutrality	point-of-view shot seen through the eyes of the Khan kids	tracking shot – they are going through Bradford in a van	The Khan kids experience Bradford from the van. It is their perspective. But they are outsiders arriving there and watching the street scene like tourists.
Leaving Salford	long shot that shows the van from a distance as it is leaving	eye-level shot	establishing shot to show the location as a whole and being left	static – the van is leaving	The contrast between Salford and the landscape the Khans will cross as well as colourful Bradford is striking. Bradford seems to promise a happier life.
At the cinema	medium shot to seize the group of the Khan family members	eye-level shot	establishing shot to get the location	static – the people move	The atmosphere is cheerful, the Khans' cousin greets his family joyfully. It is a warm and lively welcome. Ella is accepted as if she has always belonged to the community.
At the entrance of the disco	close-up of head and shoulder of the English bouncer, Tariq in the background	slight low-angle shot to show power	reverse-angle shot to show the dialogue partner	changing between the bouncer and coming guests	The bouncer does not offer a warm welcome to everyone who wants to enter the disco but he checks everybody's face and origin. People who look like foreigners are not allowed to come in.
A Bollywood romance	medium shot of the couple to show their relationship	eye-level shot: equal partners	reverse-angle shot to show the man is courting the woman	panning left towards the woman	The cliché of romantic Indian love is shown as we know it from Bollywood movies. Courting precedes love marriage. It is the man who is singing for his beloved girl who is waiting for him.
English courting	medium shot of the teens at the bar	eye-level shot: all equal	establishing shot to show the scene at the bar	zooming away to show people coming to the bar	The disco is the place for hippy-free love and sexual advances. Courting is also a female thing. Women are not waiting for their lovers but they are partly aggressively watching out for them or defending them against other female competitors.

3.3 Immigration policy

Nachdem der kulturelle Unterschied zwischen Bradford und Salford herausgearbeitet worden ist, könnten entweder vor oder nach dem Sehen der folgenden Filmabschnitte bis zur Szene, in der Meenah einen Fußball durch das Fenster und genau durch das dahinter geklebte Poster mit dem Konterfei des xenophoben Politikers Enoch Powell schießt, Hintergrundinformationen zu Bradford und der Immigrationspolitik Großbritanniens in den 70ern erarbeitet werden.
Es wird daher vorgeschlagen, diesen Unterrichtsabschnitt mit dem Cartoon auf ***Copy 9*** (als Folie auf dem Overheadprojektor) zu beginnen. Die methodische Schrittfolge für die Interpretation eines Cartoons ist einzuhalten: einer Beschreibung des Bildes folgt die Analyse der Bildelemente, um schließlich die Bedeutung abzuleiten und zu bewerten sowie mit Aufgabe 2 einen Transfer zu vollziehen.

Lösungsvorschlag zu *Copy 9*:

1. Interpret the cartoon. What does it show about the attitude of the English towards immigrants?

   The cartoon shows two men in a pub who are drinking a glass of beer while other people mingle in the background. It is not possible to identify the race or origin of the men from their appearance. This impression is reinforced by the remark made by one of them who says he can recognize that the other one must be foreign because he has got an accent. He follows this with an enquiry as to when the other one will be "going back", which obviously refers to his mother country.
   At this stage, we have already noticed from the political speech that the Khan children were watching on TV and from the posters Mr Moorhouse put in his window that there seems to have been a rather hostile attitude to immigrants in the UK in the 70s. Clearly, there were some politicians who spoke out against further immigration and even favoured a policy of repatriation, i.e. sending immigrants back to their home countries.
   The cartoon reflects this situation. For many English, it seemed to be self-evident that the people who originally came from the Commonwealth countries would eventually go back. They did not want to see the UK as a country of immigration.

2. Explain why George would prefer to live in Bradford and why he insists on Pakistani brides for his sons.

   The rather hostile attitude of many English, at least, to the extent that it is shown in the film, makes George feel uncomfortable in Salford. Every day he is confronted with Mr Moorhouse's hostility and that of other neighbours who would like to send him back to Pakistan. George concludes from this that it would not be good for his sons to stay in England and marry an English girl. Perhaps he also expects them to go back to Pakistan one day as well. At the very least, he probably hopes to be better integrated into his community if his sons marry girls from Bradford.

A cartoon – "How soon will you be going back?"

1. Interpret the cartoon. What does it show about the attitude of the English towards immigrants?
2. Explain why George would prefer to live in Bradford and why he insists on Pakistani brides for his sons.

Vocabulary to describe, analyse and evaluate cartoons	
• it is about/deals with/illustrates • in the foreground/background • the caption says/states • the cartoon/image/idea refers to/ stands for/ represents	• it symbolizes/exaggerates the idea of/criticizes/ ridicules/is directed against/intends to • I dis/like … /it touches me because • I disagree with/feel

Die folgenden Sequenzen 8 bis zu einem Teil von 10 **(En: 41:58–53:42 bzw. Deu: im Kapitel 6 beginnend bei 42:07 bis zum ersten Teil von 8: 54:28)** werden einmal gesehen und szenenweise mündlich zusammengefasst (siehe *Scene index*, S. 9). Dies kann in Partnerarbeit geschehen. Mögliche Leitfragen sind:

What does George tell Ella that night?

George informs Ella about Mr Shah and his two daughters.

Describe George's attitude to the role of a father, a wife and the kids.

He thinks that he is the only one who has a right to make decisions. "Pakistani believe if father ask son marry, son follow father instruction." He also expects his wife to live his way. If not, all of them can leave.

How does Sajid find out about the engagement?

He goes to his parents' room to use the pee bucket. When he rushes out, the toggle of his parka gets stuck in the door. He cannot move and does not dare to open the door. In this way, he accidentally overhears the conversation.

Describe the scene when the kids get up in the morning.

Cheerful music is playing. Tariq is dancing. Maneer is preaching but gets a cushion thrown at his head. Saleem and Saj are quite tired. Abdul is leaving for work. For breakfast, Ella has only got some biscuits.

What is George buying at the market?

Wedding regalia: tinsel head-dresses, clothes, two watches.

How does Stella see her relationship with Tariq? And how does Tariq see it?

She compares herself and Tariq to Romeo and Juliet. She does not want to let "the colour of your dad come between us" as she loves curry and all. Tariq seems to be a bit annoyed.

Why does Earnest not understand what he is doing for his granddad?

He greets George in Arabic while holding Enoch Powell posters for his granddad.

What does George criticize his kids for and why?

He criticizes them for not looking traditional enough. He asks Saleem why he is not wearing a suit but instead looks like a hippy. He wants Tariq to cut his hair. George feels his kids do not look very Pakistani. Perhaps he was ashamed of them not being able to speak Urdu when they were in Bradford.

What does the incident with Meenah's football play show about xenophobia?

The incident shows that xenophobia may not be the main problem for the Khans. The English kids play with Meenah and do not have any problems with her Pakistani origins. Earnest is even in love with her. All of the kids run away when she breaks the window.

Um Hintergrundwissen zu erlangen, werden die auf ***Copy 10 a–e*** bereitgestellten Texte zu Bradford, Enoch Powell, der Situation von Muslimen in Großbritannien und zur Immigration in Gruppen erarbeitet und zur Präsentation, z. B. als Poster, als szenische Interpretation, als Interview usw. aufbereitet. Dieses Mini-Projekt könnte um weitere Recherchen zu den Themen angereichert werden. Alternativ könnten die Texte, ggf. um weitere Informationen ergänzt, nur als Referate präsentiert werden.
Der abschließende Bogen wird mit ***Copy 11*** gespannt, auf der blitzlichtartig Bilder und Zitate von der indischstämmigen Einwandererfamilie Mattani in drei Generationen montiert sind, deren Erfahrungen mit denen der Familie Khan verglichen werden. Dies erlaubt ein allgemeines Resumé über die britische Einwanderungs- und Integrationspolitik von den 70ern bis in die Gegenwart. Der Text der Klausur 2 nimmt Bezug auf die Familie Mattani und könnte daher hier anschließen. Er könnte aber auch im Rahmen des o.g. Projektes mit aufbereitet werden, sofern er nicht im Rahmen des *Role plays* in *Component 4*, S. 73 ff. eingesetzt wird.

Lösungsvorschlag zu *Copy 11*:

1. Compare these photos and quotes with those from the "Getting started" page.

- also a family but three generations and only one child in the photo, whereas the Khan family consists of seven kids
- no mixed cultures but instead from one culture: Indian (roots)
- the people appear friendly but more serious
- they seem to have a wealthier background than the Khan family
- their English is sophisticated standard English in contrast to George Khan's pidgin English
- parents accept and know about their children's greater liberties in a western society, and so do not appear to want to dominate too much in contrast to George Khan

2. Then describe the immigration experience at the beginning of the 21st century in contrast to the 1970s in the UK.
Consider the political situation in the UK as well as the educational and economic backgrounds of the Khan family and the Mattani family.

- the immigration experience has completely changed: immigrants do not necessarily feel unwanted
- immigrants are more tolerant: want to take up the good things from all communities and religions; the daughter does not want to make her life more complicated than necessary → pragmatic attitude
- immigrants admire Britain, they do not feel excluded
- but: the Mattani family seems to insist on good education (language) and thus, this enables them to earn good money (home, golf club, BMWs, run family business)
- the political situation has changed: immigrants – at least from the former Commonwealth countries – are not seen as a danger to the British identity; instead the British make a difference between the origin, culture and possessions of immigrants

Who was Enoch Powell? And what did he have to do with the immigration policy of the UK in the 70s?

Present the following information. Mediate the main contents of the German text.

John Enoch Powell (1912–1998) was a British politician and a Conservative Party MP. He was controversial throughout his career and held strong and distinctive views on race, national identity, and immigration. He is best remembered for a controversial speech, in which he warned his audience about the dangers of continued, unchecked immigration from the Commonwealth to Britain, where the whites had become a persecuted minority. Because of its allusion to Virgil's quote that the Tiber would foam with blood, Powell's warning was dubbed the "River of Blood speech". According to witnesses of the speech, it was "fascinating to note what little hostility emerged from the audience." The speech with its xenophobic tendencies did not end Powell's career, but he was removed from the Shadow Cabinet. Immediately afterwards, thousands of workers went on strike in protest at Powell's sacking, carrying placards saying "Don't knock Enoch" and "Back Britain, not Black Britain". A Gallup poll showed that 74% of these asked agreed with what Powell had said in his speech. A poll in 1972 showed Powell to be the most popular politician in the country. In the United Kingdom, particularly in England, "Enoch was right" became a phrase of political rhetoric throughout the 1970s, generally employed by the far right and a racist minority. The phrase implies opposition to immigration and multiculturalism.

In August 2002, Powell appeared in the "List of 100 Greatest Britons" of all time, voted for by the public in a BBC nationwide poll.

Adapted from www.wikipedia.com

Bis zu Beginn der 60er-Jahre hatte Großbritannien eine Politik der unbeschränkten Einwanderung aller Angehörigen des Commonwealth und der Kolonien verfolgt. Dies war zum einen durch Arbeitskräftemangel begründet und zum anderen durch das noch vom Empire-Gedanken geprägte Staatsbürgerschaftsverständnis der Briten. Nachdem es bereits in den 50er-Jahren zu Unmutsbekundungen in der einheimischen Bevölkerung und z. T. auch zu gewaltsamen Übergriffen gegen die zugezogenen Westinder, Afrikaner und Inder gekommen war, versuchte man in den Sechzigern durch Gesetze, vor allem den Zuzug farbiger Einwanderer zu beschränken. Gleichzeitig sollten Anti-Diskriminierungsverordnungen die gesellschaftliche Gleichstellung der ethnischen Gruppen sicherstellen. Gegen Ende des Jahrzehnts gewann das Thema Einwanderung mit dem Zuzug einer großen Menge indisch-stämmiger Flüchtlinge aus der ehemaligen Kolonie Kenia sowie der Verabschiedung eines neueren strikteren Immigrationsgesetzes und einer rigoroseren Gleichstellungsverordnung zunehmend an Brisanz. [...]

Während manche Befürworter Powell zugute hielten, dass er sich als einziger etablierter Politiker der Ängste und Besorgnisse der einfachen Bevölkerung annahm und diesen Gehör verschaffte, warfen ihm Kritiker vor, auf niederste Weise Überfremdungsangst und Rassismus zu schüren und mit seiner blutrünstigen Metaphorik sogar fremdenfeindlichen Gewaltakten Vorschub zu leisten.

From: Tönnies, Merle/Claus-Ulrich Viol (ed.): British Political Speeches. Stuttgart, Reclam 2001, pp. 63–64

Enoch Powell: "I seem to see 'the River Tiber foaming with much blood'" – The River of Blood Speech

Present the following excerpt from the speech in an appropriate way.

A week or two ago I fell into conversation with a constituent, a middle-aged, quite ordinary working man employed in one of our nationalised industries. After a sentence or two about the weather, he suddenly said: "If I had the money to go, I wouldn't stay in this country. [...] I have three children, all of them been through grammar school and two of them married now, with family. I shan't be satisfied till I have seen them all settled overseas. In this country in fifteen or twenty years' time the black man will have the whip hand over the white man."

I can already hear the chorus of execration. How dare I say such a horrible thing? How dare I stir up trouble and inflame feelings by repeating such a conversation? The answer is that I do not have the right not to do so. Here is a decent, ordinary fellow-Englishman, who in broad daylight in my own town says to me, his Member of Parliament, that the country will not be worth living in for his children. I simply do not have the right to shrug my shoulders and think about something else. What he is saying, thousands and hundreds of thousands are saying and thinking – not throughout Great Britain, perhaps, but in the areas that are already undergoing the total transformation to which there is no parallel in a thousand years of English history.

In fifteen or twenty years, on present trends, there will be in this country 3,5 million Commonwealth immigrants and their descendants. [...] There is no comparable official figure for the year 2000, but it must be in the region of 5–7 million, approximately one-tenth of the whole population, and approaching that of Greater London. [...] As time goes on, the proportion of this total who are immigrant descendants, those born in England, who arrived here by exactly the same route as the rest of us, will rapidly increase. Already by 1985 the native-born would constitute the majority. It is this fact above all which creates the extreme urgency of action now, of just that kind of action which is hardest for politicians to take, action where the difficulties lie in the present but the evils to be prevented or minimized lie several Parliaments ahead.

The natural and rational first question with a nation confronted by such a prospect is to ask: "How can its dimensions be reduced?" Granted it be not wholly preventable, can it be limited, bearing in mind that numbers are of the essence: the significance and consequences of an alien element introduced into a country or population are profoundly different according to whether that element is 1 per cent or 10 per cent. The answers to the simple and rational questions are equally simple and rational: by stopping, or virtually stopping further inflow, and by promoting the maximum outflow. Both answers are part of the official policy of the Conservative Party.

From: Tönnies, Merle/Claus-Ulrich Viol (ed.): British Political Speeches. Stuttgart, Reclam jun., pp. 66–70

Bradford – A city of immigrants and clashing cultures?

Present the following information in an appropriate way.

Bradford is a large city in West Yorkshire with a population of nearly 300,000. The district as a whole has nearly 500,000 inhabitants. As an urban sub-area, it is the 11th largest settlement in England. Bradford is historically a working-class, ethnically-mixed city. Since its rapid growth in the 19th century, there have been several significant waves of immigration, notably Irish (19th century), Poles (1940s-50s) and South Asian people. Today, Bradford has the second highest population of Asians of any UK city, with approximately 68,000 Pakistanis, 12,500 Indians and 5,000 Bangladeshis. However, the majority of 78.3% of the people in the city are white in comparison to 18.9% Asian. Nevertheless, over the course of a few decades, the white and Asian communities have become increasingly segregated. Ethnic ghettoes have been developing within different areas of the city; for example, in 2000 the city district of Toller was 64% South Asian, Tong was 93% white, and Wibsey was 91% white.

Although the city has been praised for its cultural diversity, on occasion conflict has arisen. In January 1989, copies of Salman Rushdie's 'The Satanic Verses' were publicly burnt in Bradford, and the city's Muslim community took the lead in the campaign against the book in the UK. In July 2001, ethnic tensions and troubles in other northern towns led to serious rioting in Bradford which became known as 'The Bradford Riot'.

The Bradford Riot occurred as a result of heightened tensions between ethnic minority communities and the city's white majority, which was stoked by confrontation between the Anti-Nazi League and far right groups such as the National Front.

What began as a riot turned into a race-related disturbance, with Asians targeting businesses and cars, along with numerous attacks on shops and property and the firebombing of a white recreational centre. About 100 south Asian youths smashed windows and threw Molotov cocktails into this centre. Exits were blocked by burning cars so the occupants inside could not flee the burning building until the attackers were dispersed by riot police.

Several riots followed a few days later, when a hundred white youths attacked police and an Asian-owned Pizza restaurant was destroyed by a gang of white youths.

More than 300 people were injured, including 120 police, during the riot. 36 people (13 white and 23 Asian) were arrested. The damage caused was about £ 27 million. Sentences for the rioting were up to 6 years. It was described as 'unfortunate' that the background to the riot was stated as not being of interest to the court by the judge. In 2006, a TV fictional drama was produced that was based loosely on the riots from the perspective of an Asian family.

Adapted from: www.wikipedia.com

The Upper Globe pub was attacked during the riot and has since lain derelict.

Muslims in Britain

Present the following information in an appropriate way.

Immigration into Britain, particularly during the last 50 years, has resulted in a substantial growth of other non-Christian religions, such as Islam, Sikhism and Hinduism. The number of practitioners is growing because of relatively high birth rates in these groups and because of conversion to such faiths by young working-class non-whites and middle-class whites.

There are now 1.6 million Muslims, of whom some 665,000 regularly attend the mosque. Most have origins in Pakistan and Bangladesh, but there are other groups from India, Arab countries, Cyprus, the Middle East and Eastern Europe. The Islamic Cultural Centre and its Central Mosque in London are the largest Muslim institutions in the West, and there are mosques (1,000) in virtually every British town with a concentration of Muslim people. The Muslim Council of Britain, formed in 1997, is the umbrella representative body for most British Muslims. [...]

Non-Christian religions amount to some 1.4 million active or practicing members and represent a significant growth area when compared to the Christian Churches. But these communities constitute a relatively small proportion of the British population, 72 percent of which remains nominally Christian despite the growth of agnostics, atheists and those who claim no denominational identity. Non-Christian groups have altered the religious face of British society and influenced employment conditions, since allowances have to be made for them to follow their religious observances and customs.

They have also become vocal in expressing their opinions on a range of matters, such as protests about British foreign policy in the Middle East and Iraq; against Salman Rushdie's novel *The Satanic Verses,* parts of which are considered to be blasphemous; and Muslim claims that British law discriminates against their religion.

From: John Oakland, British Civilization. An Introduction. London, Routledge, 2006, pp. 267–269

substantial considerable

practitioner here: religiously active person
conversion the act of changing one's religion

Cyprus ['saɪprəs] Zypern
agnostic [æg'nɒstɪk] belief that it is not possible to know whether God exists or not

atheist ['eiθiɪst] belief that God does not exist
to alter to change
allowance [ə'laʊəns] here: a permitted difference
observances here: *Gebote*

Salman Rushdie famous Indian-British author
blasphemous ['blæsfəməs] insulting a religion

Muslims attend Friday prayers at Park Mosque, London on 8 July 2005

Immigration to the UK

Study the following data and present them in an appropriate way.

British-Asians in Britain

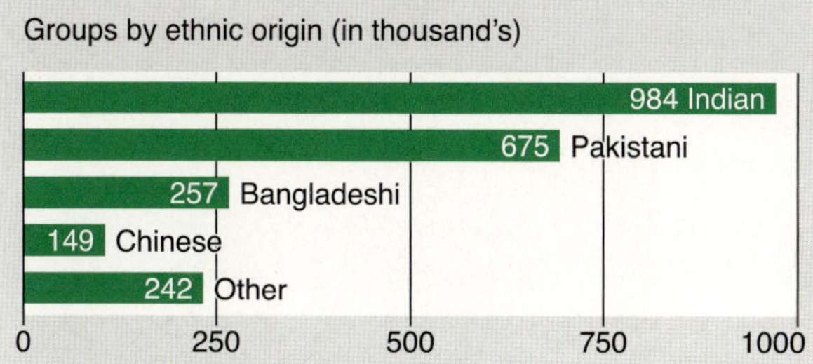

Population: Two million plus (1999)
Leicester: 30% non-white
Prediction: Europe's first non-white majority by 2011?

Data: National Statistics, 2000

Population by ethnic group, 2001

No. in 1000s/(Percentage)					
White	54,154	(92,1)	Black or Black British	1,149	(2,0)
All ethnic minorities	4,635	(7,9)	Black Caribbean	566	
Asian or Asian British	2,331	(4,0)	Black African	485	
Indian	1,053		Black other	98	
Pakistani	747		Chinese	247	(0,4)
Bangladeshi	283		Other groups	231	(0,4)
Other Asians	248		Mixed	672	(1,1)

The new blacks

% of respondents saying their neighbourhood would disapprove if more people from the following groups moved in:

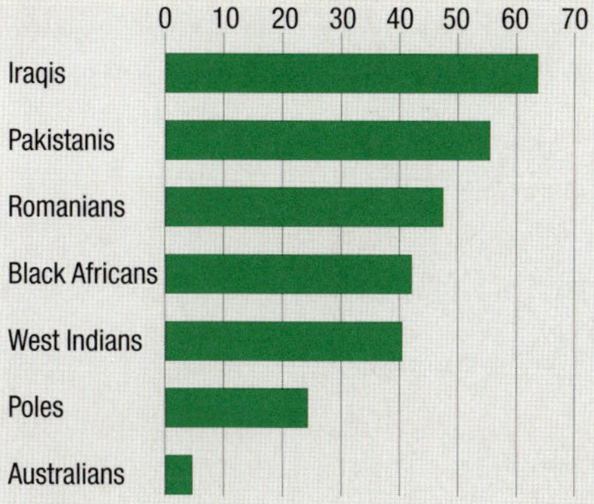

Respondents were asked whether they thought too many immigrants were coming to Britain. To the 74% who said yes, the following question was put:
Which of these is the biggest problem caused by too many immigrants coming to Britain?

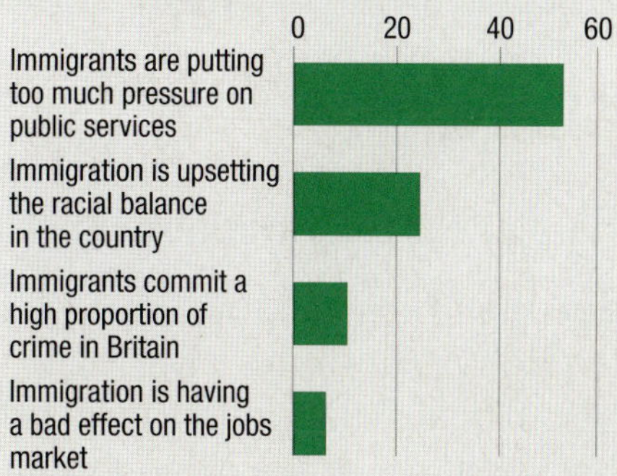

Data: YouGov
YouGov questioned 1,644 electors throughout Britain online on December 7th and 8th 2004

The Mattanis: Three generations, two cultures

The Mattani family home in Leicester, now holding three generations, has a relaxed sense of 'let's get on with it without fuss or conflict'. It's a happy home next door to one of the city's golf clubs. The area has a distinctive sense of affluence, with BMWs or similar cars parked in most of the drives. For the Mattanis the comfort has come through hard and long hours to make it happen, the Asian way.

"What we've learned is that it's important to take up the good things from all communities and religions. We'd like to pass that onto our daughters as well."
Hemant and Priti Mattani

"I'm a British businessman with Indian roots. My daughter's a British-Indian because the Indian roots are there ... There are good things in there."
Hemant Mattani

"You've got these cultural differences. Why make your life more difficult? I think, they'd prefer it if I was with somebody from my community ... I'd like to continue living in an extended family because I like living with my grandparents and mum and dad."
Shefali Mattani

Priti Mattani: Runs the family business with Hemant

"You don't have much choice now. At 12 they threaten to call some of these action lines or parent lines to complain. At 16 they get their provisional driving licences and at 18, they say, they're going to do what they're going to do! ... At the end of the day, it is their decision."
Hemant Mattani

"I want to salute Britain. To accept so many different people, it needed to have something. And that is tolerance, and I admire Britain for that."
Chandu Mattani

Chandu Mattani: A quarter century of success

1. Compare these photos and quotes with those from the "Getting started" page.
2. Then describe the immigration experience at the beginning of the 21st century in contrast to the 1970s in the UK.
   Consider the political situation in the UK as well as the different educational and economic backgrounds of the Khan family and the Mattani family.

Component 4

"Love is a question of time" – Marriage and family

4.1 Vorbemerkung und Einstieg

Dieser Unterrichtsbaustein, der die **Filmsequenzen 10 bis 13 (Deu: Kapitel 8 und 9)** umfasst, ist dem Themenbereich „Liebe, Heirat, Familie" gewidmet. Es wird dabei auch Bezug auf Filmszenen, wie z. B. Nazirs Flucht vor der Heirat, genommen, die zum Thema passen und bislang nicht detailliert besprochen worden sind. Die filmtechnische Analyse fokussiert u. a. auf die Körpersprache und den Soundtrack.

Haben die Schüler in *Component 2* die *Character map* und das *Character sheet* erarbeitet, so bietet sich die Präsentation der Ergebnisse nach der Behandlung von Sequenz 13 an, um z. B. das unter Punkt 4.3 vorgeschlagene Rollenspiel eines *Family council* der Familie Khan vorzubereiten. Alternativ ist eine Talkshow zum Thema „Is love a question of time? – Love versus arranged marriages" möglich. Vor- und Nachteile beider Varianten werden dargelegt, sodass in Abhängigkeit von der jeweiligen Kurssituation und der Einstellung der Schülerinnen und Schüler über den Einsatz entschieden werden kann. Für die Talkshow werden Rollenkarten zur Verfügung gestellt und es wird auf ergänzende Texte verwiesen, u. a. auf den unter 4.4 vorgestellten Internet-Chatauszug, der sich darüber hinaus für kreatives Schreiben anbietet.

Mit den Standbildern auf ***Copy 12*** wird in das Thema eingeführt und zu den nachfolgenden Filmsequenzen übergeleitet.

Lösungsvorschlag zu *Copy 12:*

How do the couples look?
What do their looks tell us about their ethnic backgrounds?

Nazir and bride: traditional Pakistani clothes, Nazir with turban and tinsel and in a white-red-golden uniform-like costume, the bride in a red and golden dress with veil and jewellery → both obviously have the same Pakistani background

Tariq and Stella: both in western clothes, Tariq in white work clothes → Stella is a typical west European blond girl, Tariq's hair and face show he has another cultural background

Ella and George: George in a standard European-style suit but a traditional Pakistani cap, Ella in an elegant, British-style, purple suit with hat → George does not appear to be completely Pakistani but instead partly westernized whereas Ella's appearance is that of a British middle-class woman

What does their body language tell us about their relationships?
Do man and woman feel drawn to each other?

Nazir and bride: there is a distance between them, they do not touch

"Like Romeo and Juliet?"

Nazir and his bride

Stella and Tariq

Ella and George

Describe the stills:

- How do the couples look?
- What do their looks tell us about their ethnic backgrounds?
- What does their body language tell us about their relationships?
- Do man and woman feel drawn to each other?

About the film:

- Do you think that George's marriage to Ella was an arranged or a love marriage? Justify your answer.
- Why does George not allow his sons to choose their wives?
- How will Abdul and Tariq react if they find out about their father's matchmaking?

each other, shy looks as they have not seen each other before → the bride seems to be more curious and willing to agree with the marriage whereas Nazir looks reluctant.
Tariq and Stella: hold each other tightly, look into each other's eyes → are in love, seem to have a sexual relationship, too
Ella and George: touch each other's shoulders, feel close to each other, are laughing → their gestures show they have had a long relationship and they know each other well

Do you think that George's marriage to Ella was an arranged or a love marriage? Justify your answer.

As Ella comes from another cultural background where arranged marriages are not common or even known about and George came to England alone to work there, it can be supposed that their marriage was a love marriage.

Why does George not allow his sons to choose their wives?

Although George is married to an English woman, he is not willing to allow his sons to choose a wife, let alone one with a British origin. A major reason seems to be that George is afraid of losing his identity. One clue is given in the film when George talks to the Mullah and they decide to make George's sons join the – Pakistani – community fully to avoid any problems with the English surroundings. In addition, George does not seem to approve of English girls' attitudes to courtship and love as he ignores Stella completely.

How will Abdul and Tariq react if they find out about their father's matchmaking?

Individual answers are expected. Reasons have to be given that make reference to the two sons' characters and most likely behaviour. The guessing can be continued with speculations about the other siblings' reactions.

4.2 Sequences 10 and 11: Violence in the family

Im Rahmen von *Component 3* wurden Aufgaben zum Film bis zu **Sequenz 10, Szene 3** „Meenah breaks a window" **(Deu: Kapitel 8 bis 54:28)** gestellt. Mit der letzten Frage von *Copy 12* wird zum weiteren Filmverlauf übergeleitet. Die Schüler sollen nun ihre Vermutungen mit der tatsächlichen Filmhandlung in den **Sequenzen 10 und 11: 0:53:43–1:05:29 (Deu, Kapitel 8: 54:29–1:00:42)** vergleichen. Sie erhalten folgende Beobachtungsaufgaben für einen ersten Sehvorgang, die auch arbeitsteilig übernommen werden können, z. B. in Abhängigkeit davon, auf welche Charaktere (*Component 2*) sich die Schüler konzentrieren:

1. Observe how the Khan siblings react to the news and deal with the situation that it leads to.
2. Explain George's behaviour.

Die Ergebnisse können in Stichpunkten als Tafelbild festgehalten werden. Ergänzt wird dieses um die Antwort auf nachfolgende Aufgabe 3, die in einem zweiten Sehvorgang für einen Ausschnitt aus der **Sequenz 11: 59:57–1:02:19 (Deu: 1:00:06–1:02:24)** – nun aber ohne Bild! – bearbeitet wird. (Sollte Klausur 1 eingesetzt werden, bietet es sich ggf. an, kein Tafelbild zu erarbeiten, sondern nur mündlich zu vergleichen.)

3. Concentrate on the soundtrack. What situation is depicted on television und how does it correspond to the one in the family?

Violence in the family

Reactions of the Khan siblings to the engagement and the ongoing situation

Abdul:	not at home first, does not follow Tariq to see Nazir, thinks he can please his father if he marries the chosen bride, wants a family
Tariq:	is furious, drags all the wedding clothes out of the trunk, stamps on the watches, cannot believe that his father has organized the engagement behind his back, supposes Maneer knew about it, decides to leave later
Saleem and Meenah:	are shocked first at the news, then at Tariq's reaction, try to hinder Tariq from taking the things out of the trunk, are afraid of the worst reaction of their father, run away, follow Tariq to Eccles later
Sajid:	is afraid of Tariq's furious reaction and what might happen, runs away, observes his father beating up his brother and his Mum, is terrified
Maneer:	stays calm, denies he knew anything, is left alone with the mess and tries to arrange it all, does not tell his father anything but takes his anger upon him, is beaten up → "Gandhi": peaceful resistance

George's behaviour

- is shocked that someone has opened the trunk and destroyed the watches
- becomes furious when Maneer, his most obedient son, will not tell him who it was, feels it is a rebellion against his authority
- is not able to talk quietly to Ella but continues to hit Maneer
- becomes even angrier when Ella starts to defend the kids against his ignorance
- thinks she is not supporting him → does not know what to do as Ella does not try to de-escalate, so he beats her up and threatens to kill all of them

On television

- a kind of cartoon that deals with the loneliest planets in the universe where there is sometimes only rock = George is being shown
- one planet with little aliens, the Clangers, who feel alone on their planet = like the Khans
- the Clangers are having a party = Ella announces visitors from Bradford → parallelism: loneliness of a group; contrast: happy aliens but unhappy kids

4.3 Sequences 12 and 13: What kind of family? – How to solve the conflict

In den Sequenzen 12 und 13 wird dargestellt, wie insbesondere Tariq nach einer Lösung für die Situation sucht, während Abdul sich der Entscheidung des Vaters fügt. **Sequenz 12:**

1:05:30 – 1:08:49 (Deu innerhalb von Kapitel 8: 1:02:25 – 1:09:19) könnte, da sie in starkem Kontrast zu den vorangehenden Szenen steht und reichlich Raum für Vermutungen über Nazirs Schicksal bietet, ohne Bild gesehen werden. Die Schüler raten dann nur mithilfe des Soundtracks und der Dialoge, was passiert.

> Speculate about what happens. Who are the people? What are they talking about?

Daraufhin wird die Sequenz mit Bild gesehen und mit den Vermutungen verglichen. Es wird ein Tafelbild über die Versuche zur Konfliktlösung begonnen. Impulsfragen:

> What life has Nazir chosen? Is he happy?
> Why do the Khan siblings return home from Eccles?

How to solve the conflict

Act like Nazir?
Is gay, has a French friend who is his boss, cannot offer an alternative family life to his siblings, has to renounce his family → no solution for Tariq

Das Tafelbild wird nach dem Sehen der **Sequenz 13: 1:08:50 – 1:13:33 (Deu, Kapitel 9: 1:09:20 – 1:13:59)** weiter ergänzt. Beobachtungsaufträge:

> Why doesn't George accept Tariq's arguments for choosing his own life?
> How does Tariq answer his father's argumentation?
> Is the conflict solved? Why/why not?

Talk to his father and try to change his mind?
To make his father understand that everybody has a right to choose his own life, that he is English and not Pakistani → George is too stubborn and proud to accept his son's argumentation, probably fears losing his son, does not see the double standards of his own lifestyle being married to an English woman, threatens Tariq → no solution visible for Tariq

Accept his father's choice?
To marry a "Paki" first, then also take an English wife → Tariq attacks his father's lifestyle, reveals George's hypocrisy, thus silencing him → no final solution as the answer implies that Tariq would also leave his Pakistani wife just as his father did

4.4 Role play: Arranged versus love marriage

Vor Auflösung der Konfliktsituation in den letzten Filmkapiteln bietet sich eine freie Diskussion der Thematik „Arranged versus love marriages", ggf. als szenisches Spiel in Rollen, an. Sofern im Rahmen von *Component 2* die Aufträge zur Erarbeitung eines *Character sheets* und der *Character map* vergeben worden sind, könnten diese nun in Vorbereitung der Diskussion präsentiert werden und ggf. in eine mündliche Benotung einfließen.
Es werden im Folgenden zwei Spiel- bzw. Diskussionsvarianten zur Auswahl vorgestellt, deren Vor- und Nachteile im Anschluss an ihre Beschreibung kurz zusammengefasst werden:

1. A family council at the Khans' house

Die Schüler und Schülerinnen identifizieren sich mit einer der Filmfiguren und übernehmen deren Rolle. Im Rahmen eines fiktiven Familienrates, der einberufen wird und dem ggf. auch Nebenfiguren wie Stella Moorhouse angehören könnten, wird die Situation mit dem Vater diskutiert und nach einer Lösung gesucht. Vorteilhaft ist bei dieser Variante, dass ggf. erarbeitete Ergebnisse aus *Component 2* schlüssig aufgenommen und in einen neuen Kontext transferiert werden. Nachteilig kann sich auswirken, dass sich Schüler zu sehr an den überwiegend eindimensionalen Charakteren orientieren und zudem deren teilweise *abusive language* übernehmen. Schüler könnten auch von der Situation an sich überfordert sein, da ihnen diese kulturell unbekannt ist und sie daher zu einer klischeehaften Darstellung neigen.

2. A talk show: "Is love a question of time?"

Eine zweite Möglichkeit besteht darin, das Thema losgelöst von den Filmfiguren und im erweiterten Kontext einer Talkshow zu diskutieren. Dafür werden Rollenkarten auf ***Copy 13*** zur Verfügung gestellt. Die Rollen sind an authentische Fälle angelehnt, die u. a. in einzelnen Texten in diesem Heft gesammelt sind und die daher auch, sofern sie nicht anderweitig, z. B. als Klausur, eingesetzt werden sollen, zur Erarbeitung der jeweiligen Rollen verwendet werden können. Am problematischsten gestaltet sich in der Regel die Übernahme von Rollen, die auch positive Aspekte in einer arrangierten Ehe sehen (Rollen 3 und 8). Daher sollten diese Rollen insbesondere von eloquenten Schülern übernommen werden, um eine lebendige Diskussion abzusichern. Die Rolle des Talkmasters *(Host)* übernimmt die Lehrkraft, da sie alle anderen Rolleninhalte kennt.

	Role	Additional text	Copy/page
1	Host	Arranged, forced and love marriages (definitions)	Copy 14, p. 77
2	Mark, chatter	An Internet chat: "My loveless arranged marriage" (the perspective of an unhappily married man)	Copy 15a, p. 78
3	Janee (Medusa, Lumpy), chatter	Re: "My loveless arranged marriage" (all arguments given here by chatters)	Copy 15b, p. 79
4	Noor Khan, forced *bride*	Arranged, forced and love marriages (definitions)	Copy 14, p. 77
5	Mr. Smith, a community officer for forced marriages	Arranged, forced and love marriages (definitions)	Copy 14, p. 77
6	Hemant Mattani, British-Indian father	Barnie Choudhury: Three generations, two cultures (the father's perspective on his daughter's life)	Klausur 2, p. 23; Copy 11, p. 68
7	Shefali Mattani, British-Indian daughter	Barnie Choudhury: Three generations, two cultures (daughter on life, family and marriage)	Klausur 2, p. 23; Copy 11, p. 68
8	George Khan, Pakistani father	Character sheet and information from the film	Characters, p. 6

Der Vorteil dieser Variante besteht darin, dass weitere Aspekte der Paarfindung und Vermählung behandelt werden können, die unter Verwendung eines Standard-Sprachregisters diskutiert werden. Nachteilig ist, dass sich die Diskussion damit etwas vom Film loslöst. Soll der Filmfluss nicht unterbrochen werden, könnte diese Diskussionsvariante daher als *Post-viewing activity* in den Unterricht aufgenommen werden.

4.5 Creative writing: A loveless arranged marriage?

Wird das o.g. Rollenspiel Variante 2 nicht im Unterricht eingesetzt, kann der auf ***Copy 15a*** abgedruckte Chat eines anonymen Mannes, dessen Ehe arrangiert worden ist und der sehr unglücklich ist, als Anlass für eine Diskussion und für kreatives Schreiben dienen. Zunächst wird der Text gelesen. Die Schüler sollen dann eine Antwort formulieren. Dies kann als Hausaufgabe aufgegeben werden.

> Write an answer to the chat. Refer to the pros and cons given by the chatter. Try to give a balanced answer. Be polite.

Die Ergebnisse werden daraufhin in Gruppenarbeit gelesen und Argumente für das Weiterführen bzw. die Beendigung der Ehe gesammelt. Diese werden im Plenum vorgestellt. Erfahrungsgemäß neigen Schüler aus Idealisierung der Liebesheirat und mangelnder Lebenserfahrung dazu, eine Empfehlung für die Beendigung dieser arrangierten Ehe zu geben.
Die Antworten der Chatter auf ***Copy 15b***, die dann gelesen werden, überraschen daher und ergeben einen hervorragenden Anlass zur Reflektion des eigenen Urteils. Impulsfragen:

> Sum up the arguments in favour of continuing the marriage and the ones against it.
> Which arguments do you find convincing? Why?
> If you were the anonymous chatter, what would you do?

Role cards

Role: Host You intend for your guests to talk about the controversial issue of arranged and self-made marriages. One aim is to work out the difference between the practical union of an arranged marriage with all its advantages and its deteriorated form – i.e. a forced marriage. Another aim is to show that a self-chosen love marriage may seem desirable in western societies but may not necessarily lead to everlasting happiness. Get all guests to speak and talk about their experiences. Encourage them to give each other advice.	**Role: George Khan, Pakistani father** You are a traditional and conservative father who is convinced that you are responsible for all important decisions in the life of your children. You think that you know what is best for your sons and daughters as they would not consider important aspects such as the religious, cultural and social background as well as the economic status of their partner but might instead fall crazily in love with someone they would probably divorce soon. You want to avoid such a disaster and ensure happiness for your family.
Role: Mark, chatter You are unhappily married although you agreed to a marriage arranged by your parents. You do not like the parents of your wife nor her education and looks. You try to appreciate your wife's character but feel it is difficult as real love has not developed. You cannot imagine having children with her and you do not know how to tell your parents, your wife and her parents or how to solve the situation. As a last resort, you have decided to ask for advice in a chat-room.	**Role: Janee, chatter** You have read a chat by a man who is unhappily married because he once agreed to an arranged marriage. Now, he does not know what to do because he feels he is not falling in love with his wife as he had hoped would happen. You think he should have reflected on his decision a bit longer, but now that he is married, it would be unfair to his wife, and both their parents to divorce quickly. He should give his wife a chance. Love can develop in time.
Role: Noor Khan, forced bride One day you were told you had to marry the son of your parents' friends who lived in the Netherlands and who you had never seen before. Your brother threatened to kill you if you did not agree. So, you did not refuse to get married, and then you left for your husband's family. You were able to resist your husband's sexual advances and by chance you escaped from the house and went to the police. Now, you are afraid of your family. You do not know how your brother might react as he could see your behaviour as a violation of the family's honour.	**Role: Mr Smith, community officer for forced marriages** You are responsible for exposing forced marriages and for protecting the women who want to escape from them. Furthermore, to help re-integrate the women into their families, you go to the parents to talk to them. In addition, you try to convince the imams of the unlawfulness of such weddings. Another place where you are active is in schools. There you organize projects with boys and girls to inform them about human rights, western attitudes to marriage and a misplaced understanding of honour.
Role: Shefali Mattani, British-Indian daughter Soon you will finish school and start university. You know your parents would like you to marry someone from your social group, culture and religion. Although you are sure your parents would not force you to do so, you think this is the way to avoid many problems. Why not marry someone who has the same Indian origins as your family? You want to have a family and to be able to rely on your parents' emotional and financial support.	**Role: Hemant Mattani, British-Indian father** You are a very successful, middle-class businessman who knows that the young people of today have a lot of rights you have little control over. You want to see your daughter happy but you would prefer it if she married someone of her race, culture, and religion. In addition, you want her to keep her social status. You would not force her into a marriage but you will try to influence her choice.

Arranged, forced and love marriages – a survey

	Arranged marriage	Forced marriage	Self-made or love marriage
Arrangement process	1. choice of partners: Parents, professional matchmakers, a matrimonial insert in a newspaper 2. contact by phone and letter, exchange of photographs and more information: long-term plans, dowry 3. first meeting of the families and the couple: special food preparation, private space for the couple to talk about their future, interests, outlook on life and to find out about each other's characters 4. decision about and fixing of engagement date 5. communication between the partners 6. engagement 7. wedding → contact between two families → introduction of partners by a third party	1. choice of partners: parents 2. decision of marriage without approval of at least one of the partners, typically the bride 3. short-term preparation of the bride/ bridegroom, no negotiation possible 4. religious wedding ceremony → contact between the parents of the families and not both partners → mostly no introduction of the partners before the marriage	predominantly the potential partners decide everything themselves 1. search 2. dating, courtship 3. time spent together 4. possibly: proposal and marriage → contact between two individuals → introduction without a third party
Criteria for choice	intellectual, cultural and social compatibility: social and economic status, education and profession, religion, language, horoscope, physical appearance	cultural, religious, social compatibility and economic status	physical appearance, social status, education, aspirations, lifestyle, parents
Reasons	• to arrange a practical union between two individuals with the same social, economic and cultural backgrounds • to avoid divorce • to avoid problems in adjusting to each other's customs and traditions	the same as for an arranged marriage and • to ensure continuity within immigrant communities • to keep the traditional lifestyle and role models, especially in terms of male-female relationships	• to realize one's love and lifestyle • also to arrange a practical union between individuals with the same social, cultural, economic, religious background
Disadvantages/ problems	• little flexibility in involving people from different social groups and across different religions and languages	the same as for an arranged marriage but • violation of the bride's/ bridegroom's right to choose her/his partner • death threats and punishments if the son or daughter does not agree to the marriage	• marriage may not last for a long time because of different backgrounds, lifestyles • romanticized love fades with time and often leads to divorce

An Internet chat: "My loveless arranged marriage"

ammark: Hi,
I am a 26 year old man married to a 23 year old woman and we are living in Kuwait. I entered into an arranged marriage last August in Pakistan with this girl. Although the marriage was arranged, our blood families didn't get close. Tension always remained there between them. Anyway, my problem is that from my engagement to my wedding and until now, I have always had reservations about the girl. I have the following problems with her:

- I don't like her looks. She has acne, I feel she smells from her nose, I also feel she is overweight in some body areas.
- I don't like her educational background. She is less educated than my standards.
- I don't like her family background.

My likes about the girl

- She is good natured, forgiving and optimistic.
- She is mentally strong.

In any case, we got married but our honeymoon was spoiled. I didn't feel any heartbeat. After spending a month with the girl, I decided to come back to Kuwait, as I am working here. I wrote to www.lifetips.com then about my problem. I got the following tips:

- Give your marriage some more time. Perhaps love can grow.
- Some people decide to live in marriages without being "heart struck" in order to raise children. You can try that.
- Third, divorce is still an option. Weigh up the consequences.
- Fourth, you can make a decision not to make a decision at this time.

I opted for the fourth option. I brought her to Kuwait and now she is living with me along with my parents in a traditional Pakistani setup. Things didn't improve much after she came here. I felt as if every day is a big burden. I felt severe depression on many days. Although I treated her well physically, I couldn't resist hurting her emotionally. I feel ashamed about that. "I just can't stop thinking that I got the wrong woman". Now our marriage is 7 months old. She is not pregnant as I am insisting that unless true love develops between us, we won't have children. I am just unable to decide anything. It is a difficult time for her as well.
Sometimes, I feel pity for the girl. I also feel I can't find a girl with such a forgiving nature as her, but at the same time I can't tolerate her physical looks. As soon as I see her, my mood goes down. I always tell myself to spend just one good day with her, but have seldom succeeded. I want some advice. Should I break up the marriage or shall I continue? Please share any other tips you might have. Really appreciate your answer. Thanks.

From: www.ojar.com/view_2635.htm

Re: "My loveless arranged marriage"

Lumpy: I feel badly for you and I'm not sure how to respond. In the U.S., arranged marriages are pretty rare. Whatever you do, don't have children until you resolve your problems! It's not fair to bring them into an unhappy home. Your complaints about her seem to be a little shallow. She can always improve upon her education in the future and acne often goes away all on its own. If there's room for love to grow here, believe me the sight of her flaws and all will bring joy to your heart if you have deeper feelings. Maybe you should try and put yourself in her shoes a little bit. She's probably feeling a little overwhelmed herself. She's in a strange country, surrounded by a strange family, far from home, etc, etc. Seems like she could really use a friendly ear. These should be ideal circumstances for the two of you to strike up a friendship and get to know one another. Try showing her the sights of your country! I really think you should give your marriage more of a chance. Stay sane.

Medusa: Could you get some counseling for your depression? Some types of counseling work very quickly, and help to make small changes in key areas, that produce huge changes in other areas.
I had a semi-arranged marriage, and never learned to love the guy. I'm getting out. But I've learned a tremendous amount about myself, and I think it would be a pity to discard a relationship without growing as much as possible in the process. Good luck.

Janee: Try to give your wife a chance. The looks and education, that's shallow. If it was a prerequisite, why did you marry her? Not to jump on you, but I have a friend who was left by her husband because she was "fat and stupid". That is what he said to her face. And that's ugly. Ironically, the ex-husband has an overweight girlfriend, bigger than my friend. My point is get over those standards of yours and be supportive. Your wife is already feeling vulnerable, being in a different country, so help build her self-esteem.

From: www.ojar.com/view_2635.htm

Component 5

"The language of humour" – Drama and comedy

5.1 Sequences 14 and 15: The Shahs meet the Khans

Vor dem Sehen der nächsten zwei Filmsequenzen bis zum Eklat stellen die Schüler Vermutungen über die mögliche Konfliktlösung an.

Speculate about the ending. How will the conflict be solved?

Mit einem Verweis auf die *Getting started*-Seite *(comedy versus drama)* wird zu einer Betrachtung der komischen Elemente als Beobachtungsschwerpunkt für die **Sequenzen 14 und 15: 1:13:34–1:23:45 (Deu, Kapitel 10: 1:13:43–1:23:55)** übergeleitet. Hierfür werden die konkreten Aufgaben des auf ***Copy 16*** bereitgestellten *Viewing logs* erläutert.

- Aim: to work out how humour is produced
- Humour: the quality in something that makes it funny and makes people laugh
- Tasks:
  Write down the character(s) that dominate the chosen scene.
  What happens in the scene?
  What sentences do you consider vital for the production of humour?
  What is the character's attitude as shown by his/her behaviour and speech?
  Give an example of striking camera work that underlines the humour of the scene.
  Describe the comical effect.

Es bietet sich eine Arbeitsteilung an: a) entweder konzentriert sich jeder Schüler auf eine oder zwei Filmfiguren oder b) jeder sucht sich drei Szenen aus, die er analysiert. Die erste Szene mit Sajid sollte nach Erläuterung der Aufgabenstellung gemeinsam gesehen und gleich im Anschluss an das Sehen analysiert werden, damit die Schüler genau wissen, wie sie das *Viewing log* bearbeiten sollen.

Die Sequenzen 14 und 15 werden zweimal gesehen: ein erstes Mal ohne Unterbrechung zur Orientierung und ggf. Auswahl der Szenen. Ein zweites Mal mit Pausen, um Notizen machen zu können.

Die Ergebnisse vergleichen und ergänzen die Schüler daraufhin in Gruppenarbeit. In einem abschließenden Unterrichtsgespräch werden die erarbeiteten Ergebnisse zusammengefasst (vgl. ***Copy 16***, *Model answer,* S. 82). Weitere Impulsfragen:

Worksheet: Viewing log – "The language of humour"

Character	Action/interaction	Words/soundtrack	The character's attitudes	Example of camera work	What is the comical effect?
Sajid					
Ella, George, the Shahs					
brides, bride-grooms					

Model answer: Viewing log – "The language of humour"

Character	Action/interaction	Words/soundtrack	The character's attitudes	Example of camera work	What is the comical effect?
Sajid	crosses the street and runs into a big new car that has to stop, sticks two fingers up, realises it's the visitors, runs home	The Pakis are here!	the visitors are the Pakis, not his own family; sees the Shahs as undesirable guests	point-of-view shot: Sajid's perspective on the visitors	the usual perspectives are reversed: the Pakis are not necessarily the Khans but the Shahs who live in Bradford
Ella, George, the Shahs	greet each other in the narrow hallway, Ella's face shows she is a bit horrified at the girls' looks, adopts a posh voice to ask them to come in	Ella: Would you like to come through to the parlour?	shows off by using Standard English and Received Pronunciation to demonstrate she is not beneath her rich visitors in class	medium shot of the hallway with the visitors, George and Ella	contrast between the Khans' poverty (small house) and the Shahs' wealth (in gaudy clothes and jewellery); Ella's change of voice, words
brides, bridegrooms	see each other for the first time, both boys stand in a row up against the wall, can hardly smile	no dialogue, joking music	the girls show no emotions, Abdul and Tariq are shocked at their brides	close-up of the faces	the reaction of Abdul and Tariq to the ugly girls
George, Mr Shah	George offers the barber's chair to Mr Shah who sits in it; George raises the chair	Please. ... Is it too low? – Hm.	George offers the best place he has, is servile to allow him to sit more comfortably	full shot of the two men	a ridiculous rather than powerful impression of the two men is produced
Ella, Meenah	intend to serve tea to the visitors, Ella sitting on the sofa, Meenah going to the kitchen	E: Will you put the kettle on, luv? M: Righty-ho.	use posh standard English with a high-pitched voice	full shot of the two	obviously, both use the register of a higher class to show off
Sajid, Mrs Shah, Ella	a conversation starts that Sajid does not want to join in on, answers cheekily about his age; Ella excuses him by referring to the circumcision; George stunned at her explanation	S: Not old enough to get married, so don't ask me. E: He's just been circumcised.	Sajid shows his disinterest and refusal in a provocative manner; Ella plays the innocent, mentioning the circumcision as a reason for his behaviour	close-up: Sajid's smiling face; full shot of the two men who start laughing at Sajid's answer	Sajid in his parka between the two men seems out of place; George cannot react furiously to Sajid's provocation; Ella's strategy to explain Sajid's behaviour with the circumcision
Mrs Shah, Meenah, George, Ella	Mrs Shah points out that Meenah should wear shalwar khameeze instead of a sari; George takes the side of his visitors, although he had told Meenah to wear the sari she had got from aunt Riffat	G: Riffat bloody stupy ... Even in Pakistan women get too modern. Tradition, sees, Ella.	Mrs Shah shows her disapproval that the Khans are not traditional; George is hypocritical: does not defend his sister but agrees with the Shahs	full shot of Meenah's sari, close-up of Mrs Shah's dissatisfied face	George's hypocrisy and the way he wants to please his visitors → shows no pride but acceptance of the visitors' superior status in contrast to Ella and the kids

Annie	enters the house, smoking, pretends not to have known about the visitors; is introduced to them; shows surprise; Ella is pleased and smiles, Abdul and Tariq are smiling	Is it these two? They're bleeding gorgeous. You're lucky you two.	pretends to be positively surprised at the beauty of the brides; it is pure irony; uses her sub-standard English	full shot of Annie coming in, point-of-view shot: her glance at the brides	Annie's ironic comments reveal George's hypocrisy – the boys look stunned at her remarks; her slang demonstrates the lower social status of the Khans
Annie, Mrs Shah (Ella)	talk about the bridegrooms; Annie refers to Christianity and to her husband who does what she wants; Ella laughs, the Shahs look puzzled, George is not amused but cannot do anything	A: … good Samaritans, just like in Bible, our Peter knows how far he can go before I knock him to kingdom come.	knows she will frighten off the visitors by linking the Khans to the Bible rather than Islam and by telling them that an English husband has to follow his wife's orders and not the other way round	full shot of Annie, Mrs Shah, Ella and George	Annie plays the innocent; by referring to her own obedient husband, Annie alludes to English partnerships where not the man but the woman has the say and that does not amuse George
Khan kids (Sajid, Meenah, Maneer)	are outside the parlour: Meenah is sitting on Sajid and is bouncing up and down on him; with Maneer, they mock at the brides and are laughing	Maneer: looks like Quasimodo	find the brides ugly and the situation somehow funny; stay outside to make jokes about the visitors	full shot of them on the sofa	contrast between the hilarious atmosphere outside and the tense one inside; as the kids can be heard inside, one can suppose sth will happen
Ella, George, Mrs Shah, Mr Shah	talk about the future home of the two couples: the Shahs criticize the small room and intend to make the boys live with them → it becomes obvious the men have not discussed the practical aspects of the marriages yet, thus, have nothing to say	Mrs S: I believe in firm discipline, especially in a non-Pakistani environment. How do you manage with so many children in such little space?	Shahs do not want their daughters to live with the Khans in Salford but want them to come with them; think there's not enough space; Ella does not agree	changing close-ups and zooming in on the characters to show their faces	the growing tension in the conversation, gradually growing dislike of the women, George's and Mr Shah's inability to react → although the men demonstrate their power on the outside, it is their wives who make the final decision
Ella and the kids with Saleem	Ella does not know what to say, goes out to look for her kids; Saleem has just shown his work of art and shocked his siblings; Ella is shocked, wants to burn the thing	S: It's an example of female exploitation in art – E: You dirty little bastard. I'll art you.	Saleem is proud of his "work of art" whereas his siblings are shocked and Ella becomes furious.	close-up: work of art and the faces; full shot: when Ella tries to get the thing	the "work of art", as this comes unexpectedly; the shock in the faces; Ella's dialogue with Saleem
Ella, Saleem, kids and the Shahs	Ella gets the "thing" but in the fracas it goes whirling through the air and lands in Mrs Shah's lap. Saleem, close behind, lands at Mrs Shah's feet. She starts to scream. Saleem screams upon seeing the girls. Mrs Shah starts to insult the Khans, Ella throws them out telling them what she thinks of their arrogance and behaviour. George is stunned.	Mrs S: I will never let my daughters marry into this jungle family of halfbreeds. E: They may be halfbred but at least they're not bleeding inbred like those two monstrosities.	Ella is fed up with the whole situation: her son's work of art and the Shahs. She adopts her slang English again to tell Mrs Shah her opinion and to defend her family. Mrs Shah is shocked at this family. There are major differences between them.	high-angle shot on Saleem on Mrs Shah's foot, low-angle shot from Saleem's perspective on the girls; full shot when the women talk to each other	Ella apologises for the fact that the hair of the work of art came off in her hand whereas the vagina lies in Mrs Shah's lap; Saleem diving into the room and landing at the feet of Mrs Shah; Ella's honest and cursing words at the Shahs; her dialogue with Mrs Shah, the silent men

- Compare your speculations with the film version.
- What strikes you about these film scenes? Would you have expected such an outcome? Why/why not?
- What were the family's (Ella's, her kids') and Annie's strategies for dealing with the situation?
  - sabotage and hidden provocation
  - revelation of British impact on the Khans
  - ignorance of the visitors
- Why did the director use humour to solve the conflict?
  - comic relief of the tension built up in the scenes before
  - to make the film not too serious but entertaining and attractive to a larger audience
- Do you find the solution of the conflict in a slap-sticky manner suitable (exaggerated/misplaced)? Why?
  - individual answers are expected

5.2 Sequence 16: "I know what's best"

Im nächsten Schritt wird untersucht, inwieweit der Konflikt tatsächlich gelöst ist, wie George wohl reagieren und wie das Leben in der Familie Khan weitergehen wird.

Do you think the conflict has been finally resolved? Why/why not?
How will George react to his family's behaviour?
How will life go on for the Khan family?

Im Mittelpunkt der letzten Sequenz steht die Figur von George und das Verhalten seiner Familie, insbesondere von Ella. Mit der kombinierten Filmanalyse- und Textaufgabe auf ***Copy 17*** wird eine zu Klausur 1 analoge Aufgabe gestellt, welche deshalb als vertiefende Vorbereitung bzw. „Generalprobe" dienen kann. Die Schüler sehen die **Sequenz 16: 1:23:46–1:29:50 (Deu, Kapitel 11: 1:23:56–1:29:59)** daher mindestens zweimal, ggf. dreimal. Die Ergebnisse werden anschließend detailliert besprochen.

Lösungsvorschlag zu *Copy 17:*

1. Describe briefly what happens in the last film scene.

   George is furious and blames Ella for the disaster, who in turn accuses him of being ashamed of her and their kids. When George starts to beat her, Abdul intervenes and pulls them apart. Ella, with all the kids standing behind her in support, tells him to leave. Nevertheless, after they are alone, she takes George's side, reminding the children that he is still their father. Later, she visits George, who is working in the shop, and they reconcile their differences over a cup of tea. Abdul and Sajid decide to throw the parka away since the hood had been torn off in the family scuffle earlier. When Saj shows Saleem's 'work of art' to Earnest, Stella and her girlfriend join them. Peggy, seeing it too, is at first angry since she had been the model for it, but soon after, all of them playfully run away down the street.

2. Analyse what film-making techniques are used to show George's feelings and thoughts and his family's attitude towards him. How is empathy with George evoked? Include the given stills in your analysis.

- contrast of George's appearance and behaviour with the Shahs: quite servile, proud, quiet, calming down all and wears Jinnah cap (still 1) → demonstrates he is the wise and reflective but powerful head of his family who follows traditional rules; with his family, he is aggressive, loud, and furious at first; he does not wear the cap any more → shows his real emotions, is ashamed of his family, does not see his own faults, blames Ella for the situation (still 2)
- medium close-up of George when he is with the Shahs: he is more in the background as the two wives are discussing the matter (still 1)
- close-ups of George's face when he is with his family alone to show his anger and frustration, then his sorrow → more personal and individual, not just a Pakistani father (still 2)
- when George tries to attack Ella, the kids defend her; to George's surprise, Abdul pushes him back and tells him it is finished; Sajid starts to pummel his father with his fists – is not afraid of him
- in the ongoing conversation, the kids make clear that they are disappointed and are not willing to let their father decide anymore about their lives; George tells them he only wants the best for them
- his family is shown standing together as a united group opposite him: Meenah's, Maneer's and Tariq's faces express sorrow, disappointment; Ella is weeping and bowing her head down → they are not against him but can hardly accept his ignorant and aggressive behaviour; they do not attack him but simply defend Ella against him (still 3)
- Ella reveals George's hypocrisy: that he is ashamed of his own family and is not interested in his children's happiness, if he cannot accept them as they are, he should leave → George is not furious any more but shocked at the situation, helpless (still 2)
- when alone with the kids, Ella reminds them that George is still their father and that she does not want to hear any curses → she is with him, does not want the kids to become alienated from him but instead to accept him
- they reconcile their differences over a cup of tea → it is like a ritual for them, a very English one

3. Which aspects of George's character as described in the extracts from one film review and an interview with Om Puri, the actor of George Khan, fit in with this sequence? Give reasons for your judgment.

- authoritative, dominant and physically abusive father: is mostly shown in the scenes with Ella (Tariq, Maneer in other sequences) → she has got a black eye
- he does not know how to react to the challenges of the English culture, which shows his limitations and his frustration
- on the other hand, he reconciles his differences with Ella over a cup of (English) tea → has adopted parts of a British lifestyle, has mar-

ried an English woman but does not allow his sons to marry one, which shows his contradictory attitudes
- not a monster → shows concern and sorrow after the final aggressive scene, is shocked that his family wants him to leave
- the lines in the script alone could make George one-dimensional but Om Puri plays him with subtleness, fine facial expressions and sudden changes of feelings so that the audience can see and feel for the character

4. Imagine how life will go on for the Khans. Will George have learnt a lesson?

Individual answers are expected. Reasons should be given.
- playful ending for the kids and their English friends
- reconciliation of Ella and George

Insbesondere mit den in *Component 6* vorgeschlagenen Materialien zum autobiografischen Hintergrund des Filmes kann die Charakterisierung von George wie auch die Darstellung der Familienkonstellation weiter vertiefend besprochen werden.

"I know what's best"

Om Puri, the actor of George Khan, about the character:

When I first read "East Is East", my first impression was, 'it's a one-dimensional character.' He's an authoritative father: mean, bashes up his children, bashes up his wife, one-dimensional. But then after a couple of readings, I started digging. There is a subtext: the man has been married to this woman 25 years. This woman is not meek. She is not timid that she will take it lying down. So there has to be something more in it. I wanted to bring out his limitations, his contradictions, his frustration, his complexity, all that. So that he is a well-rounded character. [I wanted] to make him human – he is not inhuman. He is not a monster – that was a bit of a challenge. If I had replayed it, and made him absolutely dark, you would not defend him one inch. You would say, 'No he is a monster That's it.'

meek very quiet, gentle, unwilling to argue

From: Om Puri: The soul of India, by Jeffrey M. Anderson
www.combustiblecelluloid.com/intompuri.shtml

The most powerful performance belongs to Om Puri, although his character, George, is little more than a one-dimensional monster. As written, this isn't a very interesting person, but Puri invests him with a degree of humanity and a kind of dignity.

to invest sth/sb with sth to give sb the power to do sth
dignity sense of your own worth

From: James Berardinelli, 2000
www.popmatters.com/film/reviews/e/east-is-east.shtml

1. Describe briefly what happens in the last film scene. (Comprehension)
2. Analyse what film-making techniques are used to show George's feelings and thoughts and his family's attitude towards him? How is empathy with George evoked? Include the given stills in your analysis. (Analysis)
3. Which aspects of George's character as described in the extracts from one film review and an interview with Om Puri, the actor of George Khan, fit in with this sequence? Give reasons for your judgment. (Evaluation)
4. Imagine how life will go on for the Khans. Will George have learnt a lesson? (Comment)

Film stills

Still 1
(from sequence 14)

Still 2
(from sequence 16)

Still 3
(from sequence 16)

Component 6

Post-viewing activities

6.1 The autobiographical background of the film

Auf *Copy 18a* ist ein leicht gekürztes Interview mit dem Autor des Dramas und des Drehbuchs, Ayub Khan-Din, abgedruckt, auf *18b* ein weiterführender Artikel von ihm. Khan-Din beschreibt hier den autobiografischen Charakter des dem Drehbuch und Film zugrunde liegenden Dramas und erläutert insbesondere die Motive für das Verhalten seines Vaters. Die Schüler und Schülerinnen lesen zunächst das Interview, fassen die wesentlichen Aussagen pro Abschnitt zusammen *(State the main contents of Ayub Khan-Din's answers.)* und tauschen Eindrücke dazu aus. Im Folgenden einige kurze Hintergrundinformationen zu zwei Referenzen im Interview:

David Niven (1910–1983) was an English actor, best known for major roles in *Around the World in Eighty Days* (as Phileas Fogg, 1956) and *The Pink Panther* (1963).

Indo-Pakistani war: Since the creation of the Republic of India and the Islamic Republic of Pakistan in 1947, there have been three major wars and one minor war between the two states. These have mainly been about the Kashmir region, but in the war of 1971, the war was about East Pakistan, which was declared independent and became the state of Bangladesh with the support of India. It is this third Indo-Pakistani war that the film *East is East* makes reference to.

Anschließend wird der Artikel auf *Copy 18b* entweder

a. von den Schülern als Interview aufbereitet und inszeniert

b. oder er wird mit den angegebenen Aufgaben in Vorbereitung z. B. auf eine Textklausur bearbeitet. Die Lösungen der Textarbeit werden hier in Stichpunkten der besseren Vergleichbarkeit wegen wiedergegeben.

Lösungsvorschlag zu *Copy 18b*:

1. Point out the reasons given for Ayub Khan-Din to write an autobiographical stage play.

- mother diagnosed with Alzheimer's disease; Khan-Din felt like whole sections of his life were beginning to disappear with her memory → he wanted to keep the memory of his childhood, the story of a whole family
  the neighbourhood he grew up in, Ordsall in Salford, was being demolished and the whole community was about to be broken up → wanted to capture the spirit of the area and the people he had grown up with and to discover how that world had influenced the way he was brought up
  wanted to create a decent part for himself as he was fed up with seeing the crap stereotypical roles dished out to Asian actors: corner shop owner, victim of skinheads, BLACK ACTOR

Mark Olden: A quick chat with Ayub Khan-Din

How did you get into writing?

When I left school mid 70s, I was thick as two short planks. [...]. So I got me a job as a hairdresser and I was the worst hairdresser in Manchester. I never got further than sweeping the floor and washing people's hair. One day, in the hairdressers, I picked up David Niven's book, *The Moon's a Balloon,* and read that he went from being in the army to being an actor. So I thought if someone can go from one diverse job to another, why can't I? So I just rang the local college, Salford Tech, and asked if they did a drama course. They asked what qualifications I had and just laughed. But I got in and started writing *East is East* there.

thick as two short planks *(infml)* very stupid

Salford Tech technical college in Salford

Just how autobiographical is *East is East*?

The parents are drawn directly from my own family. The youngest boy, Sajid, is me as a child. All the arguments in the film, all the theories behind the father's way of thinking, are my own arguments and theories which I developed from writing the first draft of the stage play to the last draft of the screenplay.

Among the film's running themes are the India-Pakistan war and Enoch Powell. Are they particularly vivid memories for you?

When all these events started happening, I was Sajid. I was living in a parka. Enoch Powell was always being thrown in my face as a child, and the whole Bangladesh war of independence had a big effect on our household, because what happened in the house always revolved around the TV news.

to revolve around [rɪˈvɒlv] here: to have sth as the main focus

Do you have any expectations of how the film will be received in the more traditional parts of the Asian community?

I've made a point in the film of not making it offensive or irreligious at all, so there's nothing they can point to. It's like walking on egg shells. I'm sure people will have some criticism about how I portray my father. But at the end of the day, I'm portraying my father, he's not a Pakistani everyman. To a certain extent, this is a man who abandoned his culture und married an English woman, und then decided that his children should marry Pakistanis.

offensive [əˈfensɪv] rude, insulting
irreligious [ˌɪrɪˈlɪdʒəs] showing no respect for religion

Do you think the pressures on young Asians living between the pull of different cultures are less severe than when you were growing up?

To a certain extent it's gone full circle. In Bradford it's gone from being traditional to being modern, and back to being traditional again. Because Pakistanis have not seen themselves accepted in this country und have faced racism, along with unemployment und riots, the younger generation has rebelled against the older one and said that they have become too modern and too accepting. You have to find a balance. When you decide to move to a country, you have to understand that your children are going to be influenced by the culture of that country. [...] There will always be traditional families und there will always be the kind of problems my brothers und sisters faced. It'll never go away.

riot [ˈraɪət] a group of people who behave in a violent way in a public place

From: www.kamera.co.uk/interviews/ayubkhandin.html

Ayub Khan-Din about the autobiographical parts of his stage play and the film

I wrote the first draft of my autobiographical stage play *East is East* fifteen years ago when I was at drama school. I started to write it for various reasons, the main one being that my mother had just been diagnosed with Alzheimer's disease und suddenly, as the disease progressed, it felt like whole sections of my life began to disappear with her memory. At the same time, the neighbourhood I grew up in, Ordsall in Salford, was being demolished und the whole community was about to be broken up. I wanted to capture the spirit of the area und the people I had grown up with; to discover how that world had influenced the way my mother und father brought us up. One other important consideration, particular to me at the time, was that I wanted to create a decent part for myself. I was fed up of seeing the crap stereotypical roles dished out to Asian actors: you either ran the corner shop or were a victim of skinheads. I had no idea after leaving drama school that I would suddenly be stamped with an invisible mark that said BLACK ACTOR! [...]

It was important to me from the early stages that this shouldn't be just one son's story but the story of a whole family, and not just an excuse for Paki-bashing my father (although this would have been easy to do as he did behave monstrously at times). But the more I looked at my parents und their relationship, especially considering the times they lived in, the more admiration I felt for their bravery. This was not a time of mixed-race marriages, which were barely acceptable in the middle-class salons of London. Anywhere else in Britain a white woman with a black man would be considered a prostitute. It must have been very hard for them, the hatred and bigotry they would have faced. But what I realised after looking at them from an adult perspective is what an incredibly strong relationship it created.

So why did this man who was married with a first wife und two daughters in Pakistan, who settled here in the early 1930s und married an English woman, who proceeded to have ten children whom he allowed to celebrate Christmas und Easter, why then did he decide that they could only marry Pakistanis? We never confronted him with his hypocrisy, we were too scared of him. You just didn't question him about anything; you did what he told you to do. I remember him when I was younger being playful with us, but all that changed by the age of ten. You were his son und you obeyed him, you suddenly lost all freedom of choice in any important life decisions. His relationship with my mother varied with whatever problem he was having with any of the kids and, as there were ten of us, there was always someone he was having a problem with. She always seemed to be right in the middle of it, her loyalty torn between her husband and her kids. Always trying to take our side when she could, but knowing she would inevitably bear the brunt of his anger and in the end lose another child as they were banished from the house for not toeing the party line. [...]

The more I looked at the life we led, the more it made me question my father's motives. Why was he so insistent about stamping out any spark of independence he saw in his children? I think part of his problem was that he always seemed slightly embarrassed by us in the company of his family, who had settled over here. Perhaps it was a sense of shame und guilt that this was what he'd left his first wife und daughters for. I fear we didn't come up to scratch and were a constant disappointment. In many ways he must have felt extremely isolated und would have liked to have lived in a Pakistani community like Bradford. But that was one thing my mother was quite adamant about: we were staying in Salford.

That was more or less the sum total of our Pakistani life: trips to Bradford every first Sunday in the month visiting relations, being dragged in and out of people's houses, eating curry, going to another house and eating more curry. Being given money and my dad making us give it back – which we, ever so reluctantly, did. We were never allowed to accept it. [...]

The climax of these visits would be a trip to my cousin's cinema. He looked and dressed like a film star with perfectly Brylcreemed hair und a suit, cut to perfection, which had

Alzheimer's disease ['æltshaɪməz] [dɪzi:z] illness that causes loss of memory
to demolish [dɪ'mɒlɪʃ] knock down, destroy

crap [kræp] (*sl*) bad
dish out to sb (*infml*) to give

to bash [bæʃ] (*infml*) to criticize strongly

bigotry ['bɪgətri] expression of unreasonable, esp. racist, beliefs

hypocrisy [hɪ'pɒkrəsɪ] behaviour in which sb pretends to have moral standards that he/she does not actually follow
loyalty ['lɔɪəlti] quality of being faithful
to bear the brunt of sth [brʌnt] to receive the main force of sth unpleasant

to toe the party line (*infml*) to do what sb in authority tells you to do

to come up to scratch to be as good as expected
adamant ['ædəmənt] determined not to change one's mind

Brylcreem [ˌbrɪlkri:m] a type of oil used on hair to make it shiny

a sheen to it that you could see your face in. [...] Then into the cinema: the best seats in the house and whatever Bombay film we wanted to watch. [...]
This was our Pakistani life; this was how we existed outside of Salford. A life none of my friends knew or could understand. I think in the film I came as close as possible to understanding my father's motivation in the way he tried to bring us up.

a sheen soft, smooth, shiny appearance

From: East is East. A Screenplay (Introduction). Royal Court Theatre, 1996

1. Point out the reasons given for Ayub Khan-Din to write an autobiographical stage play. (Comprehension)
2. Describe how Ayub Khan-Din sees his parents' relationship. (Comprehension)
3. Analyse the motives of the author's father for not allowing his children any independence and a life of their own. (Analysis)
4. Examine the author's attitude to Bradford and his Pakistani relatives. Refer to content and language and give evidence from the text. (Analysis/Evaluation)
5. Assess what parts of the film you can understand better after having read this article. Give reasons for your answer. (Comment)

2. Describe how Ayub Khan-Din sees his parents' relationship.

- admiration for their bravery as this was not a time of mixed-race marriages; barely acceptable in London middle-class – a white woman with a black man would have been considered a prostitute
- his parents had to face hatred and bigotry
- they developed an incredibly strong relationship
- relationship with the mother varied with whatever problem Khan-Din's father was having with any of the kids
- she always seemed to be right in the middle of it: her loyalty torn between her husband and her kids, always trying to take the kids' side when she could, but knowing she would inevitably bear the brunt of her husband's anger and in the end lose another child as they were banished from the house for not toeing the party line

3. Analyse the motives of the author's father for not allowing his children any independence and a life of their own.

- partly, it was hypocrisy
- partly, he seemed slightly embarrassed by his kids in the company of his family, who had settled in Britain; a sense of shame and guilt that this was what he'd left his first wife and daughters for → his father seems to have been seen as an outsider by the Pakistani community in Britain for having started to adapt too much to a British lifestyle; also there may have been feelings of a bad conscience as he had left his first family in Pakistan and did not intend to go back there or to let them come over to England, primarily because his English wife did not want them there
- the kids didn't come up to scratch and were a constant disappointment → they did not follow the traditional rules of behaviour, of the Muslim religion, were not acculturated to a Pakistani life in Britain, seemed to be influenced too much by the English environment and not much willing to adapt to another culture
- father felt extremely isolated and would have liked to have lived in a Pakistani community like Bradford but the mother refused to move there → the father seemed to have neither been completely integrated into the British nor the Pakistani communities, so there seems to have been a lack of identity; by marrying an English woman who refused to move to Bradford, he had given up his culture and partly his identity, too, which he seemed to recognize only gradually as his children grew up

4. Examine the author's attitude to Bradford and his Pakistani relatives. Refer to content and language and give evidence from the text.

- trips to Bradford every first Sunday in the month visiting relatives, being dragged in and out of people's houses, eating curry, going to another house and eating more curry → enumeration of activities that demonstrate the hospitality of the Pakistani community
- being given money and my dad making us give it back – which we, ever so reluctantly, did → description of behaviour that shows the generosity of relatives and his father's pride

- climax of these visits: a trip to a cousin's cinema; he looked und dressed like a film star with perfectly Brylcreemed hair and a suit, cut to perfection, which had a sheen to it that you could see your face in → euphemism of the description that shows admiration
- cinema: the best seats in the house und whatever Bombay film we wanted to watch → positive description of hospitality, shows admiration und appreciation
- A life none of my friends knew or could understand → contrast to show that somebody who has not experienced such a life would not be able to understand and give up stereotypical images

→ The author appreciates having taken part in the life of the Pakistani community even if this only happened once a month. As an adult, he can understand better why his father behaved hypocritically in his kids' perception. Khan-Din tries to overcome the stereotypical images and prejudices that the English have of the immigrant community.

5. Assess what parts of the film you can understand better after having read this article. Give reasons for your answer.

Individual answers required. Possible issues:

- the Pakistani community
- Ella's and George's relationship
- George's attitude towards his kids
- the English people's attitude towards mixed-race relations

6.2 Analysing and writing a film review

Eine weitere oder andere Möglichkeit ist die Behandlung einer Filmrezension. Die Strukturanalyse der auf ***Copy 19*** bereitgestellten Filmrezension bereitet dabei den Entwurf einer eigenen Kritik vor. Zur sprachlichen Vorbereitung könnte passendes Vokabular aus der Rezension herausgesucht werden.

Lösungsvorschlag zu *Copy 19:*

Examine the review and work out the main structure of it.

l. 1– l. 3: introduction, reference to film genre, first assessment
l. 4– l. 8: summary of setting and characters
l. 9– l. 14: plot (what happens and why?)
l. 14–l. 18: atmosphere created in the film (funny, poignant, harsh)
l. 19–l. 29: evaluation of film-making and cast with examples
l. 30–l. 34: assessment of possible success in America
l. 35: final evaluation

Bei entsprechendem Zeitvolumen oder als Hausaufgabe könnten die Schülerinnen und Schüler weitere Informationen bzw. passendes Vokabular aus anderen Rezensionen (als Vorbereitung für die eigene Kritik) sammeln und zusammentragen.

Frank Swietek: A film review

Examine the review and work out the main structure of it.

Rarely has a film blended earthy humor with powerful drama as effectively as this marvelous filmization of Ayub Khan-Din's semi-autobiographical play by the young Irish director Damien O'Donnell. The story is a conflict-of-generations tale, set in a London suburb in 1971, and centered on a Pakistani immigrant, George Khan (Om Puri), who has married a British wife, Ella (Linda Bassett); together they run a small fish-and-chips shop. They've also managed, over the years, to have a large brood of children, from the eldest son Nazir (Ian Aspinall) down to the youngest, Sajid (Jordan Routledge), who's apparently Khan-Din's surrogate.

The difficulty that the close-knit, but frequently battling family members face, at a time when anti-immigrant feelings are growing in British society as a whole [...], is that George is determined to maintain Pakistani customs, especially when it comes to the futures of his sons, whom he intends to marry off in traditional arranged marriages. It's the rebellion of his children against his dreams und desires that acts as a catalyst for the comedy and the drama of the piece. Much of the film is decidedly funny, as George's expectations come up against the realities of swinging London in the seventies. Some is poignant, as the children seek to find ways to get around him. And, especially toward the close, there are incidents that are shockingly harsh, especially when the patriarch turns violent as his family opposes his plans.

What's astonishing about "East is East" is how beautifully all this material hangs together, despite the enormous variations in tone it entails. Much of the credit must go to the fine cast, especially Om Puri und Linda Bassett. The former brings George to life with extraordinary skill; the father becomes a figure whom a viewer can sympathize with while still understanding the fear und resentment his children feel toward him. Bassett is equally amazing as his long-suffering spouse (he never neglects to remind her that he still has a first wife in Pakistan he can go back to). Her attempts to mediate between her husband and her kids are expertly caught, and when at the end Ella must suffer George's wrath and defend the interests of her children against him and the in-laws he would bring into the family, the effect is both very funny und remarkably real. The young actors playing the Khan siblings are uniformly appealing und capable [...].

"East is East" will probably be a fairly hard sell to American audiences, who will be mostly unfamiliar with the English historical context and, with their love of big-budget action flicks, are never inclined to embrace smaller films that have the courage to be more complex than the feel-good foreign pieces of whimsy that usually succeed on these shores. One can only hope that it will buck the odds and gain wide acceptance; it's both an exceptionally funny and quite affecting film.

From: www.popmatters.com/film/reviews/e/east-is-east.shtml

surrogate ['sʌrəgət] a person or thing that takes the place of sb/sth else

catalyst ['kætəlɪst] sb/sth that causes a change
poignant ['pɔɪnjənt] *ergreifend*
the close here: the end
an incident ['ɪnsɪdənt] sth that happens
patriarch [ˌpeɪtri'a:k] male head of a family who makes all decisions
to entail [ɪn'teɪl] to involve unavoidably
the credit praise
resentment [rɪ'zentmənt] *Groll*

wrath [rɒθ] *(arch)* extreme anger
the in-laws *(infml)* relatives by marriage

a flick *(infml)* a film
whimsy *Laune, Spleen*
to buck the odds here: *die Verkaufszahlen sprengen*

Eine ganze Reihe informationsreicher und interessanter Kritiken, unter anderem zur Werbe-Strategie und zum Filmgenre, sind zu finden unter http://ofcs.rottentomatoes.com/movie-1096281/reviews.php. Hervorzuheben sind die Artikel folgender Autoren: James Berardinelli, Damian Cannon, Karina Montgomery, Eugene Novikov, Eric D. Snider.

6.3 Writing a screenplay

Dieser Unterrichtsvorschlag geht über den engeren Inhalt des Films hinaus, will aber in Anlehnung an die Themen des Films zum kreativen Schreiben anregen. Die Schüler sollen einen eigenen Drehbuchausschnitt entwerfen. Eine Anleitung dazu wird auf ***Copy 20*** bereitgestellt. Neben dem hier abgedruckten Beispiel einer (gekürzten) Schülerarbeit, sind eine ganze Reihe weiterer von Schülern des Angergymnasiums Jena erstellte Arbeiten zu finden unter www.wiki.klemm-site.de/wiki/index.php.

The two characters are 19-year-old Ayub and his 16-year-old sister Saeeda who live in Salford. Ayub is secretly engaged to Annie and intends to marry her son.

1. INT. FLAT IN SALFORD – 1ST APRIL, MORNING

Camera follows SAEEDA, who walks down the stairs and enters the kitchen. AYUB sits there eating his breakfast.

AYUB:
Good morning. Did you sleep well?
SAEEDA:
Yeah, fine.
AYUB:
Coffee?
SAEEDA:
Thanks.
AYUB:
With milk?
SAEEDA:
Er, milk? Yes please.

AYUB pours the milk in her cup, then tries to ignore SAEEDA and reads the newspaper very intensively.

AYUB:
I need to go to town to get the engagement ring for Annie.
SAEEDA:
Oh, my goodness! You plan to marry that girl. You hopefully know what dad will do with you if you tell him. *(looks at the ceiling)* Allah bless you.
AYUB:
Thanks for your help. Of course I know how dad will react, but it is definitely not your task to tell him. *(mumbles)* Your luck!
SAEEDA:
But you haven't already made any plans about the marriage, have you?
AYUB:
Don't know.

SAEEDA:
Ayub? Tell me the truth? Have you done anything?

AYUB:
Oh, Saeeda. I love this woman and I don't want to meet her secretly. I don't want to keep quiet. All people should know that I'm in love with Annie. And daddy … I don't give a damn shit!

SAEEDA:
(interrupts) Okay. Your marriage is planned. And perhaps the day is already chosen.

AYUB:
Yes, it is.

SAEEDA:
Well, and when is it?

AYUB:
We have chosen the 20th April. It's the best day. It's spring, so we can sit in the garden. And it is not too warm and not too cold. It's the perfect day to …

SAEEDA:
(interrupts) … Oh no! That's the birth of the prophet, the most important Pakistani feast. You can never marry on this day. Remember, our family will be in Bradford to visit our relatives.

AYUB:
Shit. I forgot it. Yes, I just forgot it.

SAEEDA:
Got a bad break, hm? You have to change the date! But it would be better to cancel the whole marriage. You know exactly what daddy's opinion is about a marriage between an English woman and one of his beloved sons.

AYUB:
That gets on my nerves. I am going to marry Annie. Nobody can mess with my decision. So, now I have to go to town to buy the engagement ring. Some recommendations for the ring? Simple or pompous?

Abridged from: www.wiki_schoolmaster.de, by Kristin and Diana

In einem weiteren Schritt könnten die Schüler sich gegenseitig ihre *Screenplays* vorstellen, um sich dann auf die szenische Darstellung ausgewählter Beispiele zu einigen.

Method sheet: How to write a screenplay

1. Task: Write an extract of a screenplay, either

a. of one scene that you create for the film *East is East,* or
b. of a scene taking up an issue from the film but with your own characters.

2. How to start: First, draw a sketch.

a. **General structure** of a screenplay:
- a set-up: introduction of characters and their goals
- the main part, in which the hero/heroine meets some kind of opposition
- the ending when the problems are resolved

b. **Synopsis:** First write down the synopsis or summary of the action that is going to take place. Consider setting, conflict and characters.

c. **Setting:** Decide on the place (country, town or village), the time (century, decade), the social background (lower, middle, higher class).

d. **Conflict:** Drama and a movie are based on conflict, such as an unhappy romance, match-making for a marriage, a failed exam, an unsatisfying relationship, etc. Your characters will have to deal with obstacles and look for solutions.
- What kind of conflict/obstacle do your characters have to face?
- Who stands in the way and why?
- How do(es) the protagonist(s) try to achieve his/her/their goal(s)?
- Which attempts will fail, which ones will be successful? Why?
- What does the hero learn that may teach something to the audience?

e. **Characters:** The characters are involved in some kind of conflict as protagonist(s) and antagonist(s). They don't necessarily need to be "enemies". Consider the following aspects when you create characters:
- name (symbolical meaning!) and age
- special character traits (some can be strange!)
- home (flat, house) and family (status, siblings, pets, etc.)
- best friends, relations (at school, at work, in clubs, etc.)
- likes, dislikes, hobbies, favourite activities, etc.

f. **Props, camera work:** Think of appropriate props and reflect on the shots.

3. How to proceed: Work out the screenplay in detail.

EACH SCENE STARTS WITH A **SLUG LINE** WRITTEN IN CAPITAL LETTERS THAT GIVES INFORMATION ABOUT TIME AND PLACE (EXT. = EXTERIOR, INT. = INTERIOR).
EXAMPLE: EXT. ROAD BRADFORD – NIGHT, 10. p. m.

Then you give **instructions for the action** that is going to take place with information on **camera settings** and **movements**.
Example: Muhammad starts to climb out of the window of his house. Low-angle shot. Behind him, his younger brother, in his bed, is looking at him. Over-the-shoulder shot.

CAPITALIZED NAMES OF THE CHARACTERS AT THE **CENTRE** OF THE PAGE.
EXAMPLE: MUHAMMAD

The dialogue **is indented** and there are **no quotation marks**: You won't say anything, will you? You'll get some sweets.

Weiterführende Materialien

Medien zum Film und Webbiografie

Khan-Din, Ayub (1996): *East is East. A Screenplay.* Royal Court Theatre.

Khan-Din, Ayub (1999): *East is East. Film Script.* London: Film Four Books.

O'Donnell, Damian (1999): *East is East. DVD,* Film Four.

http://ofcs.rottentomatoes.com/movie-1096281/reviews.php (Website der *Online Film Critics Society* mit 17 Filmkritiken zu *East is East)*

www.combustiblecelluloid.com/intompuri.shtml (Jeffrey M. Anderson: Om Puri: The Soul of India, 2000)

www.kamera.co.uk/interviews/ayubkhandin.html (Mark Olden: A Quick Chat with Ayub Khan-Din)

www.english.emory.edu/Bahri/Khan1.html (Website von Tina Bhatnagar von der Emory University mit Informationen zu Ayub Khan-Din, den *major issues* des Films und Internetquellen, 2000)

www.wiki.klemm-site.de/wiki/index.php (von Uwe Klemm, einem Gymnasialschullehrer aus Jena betreute Schüler-Wikipedia, mit Beiträgen aus dem Unterricht, u.a. einem Projekt zum Film)

Weiterführende Quellen, Informationen und Unterrichtshilfen

Kestermann, Thomas (2002): „Identitätsfindung zwischen Fremd- und Selbstbestimmung in ‚East is East' (1999)", in: *Der Fremdsprachliche Unterricht Englisch,* 5/2002, S. 25–31.

Labi, Aisha: The Runaway Bride, *TIME,* May 5, 2003, p. 38–41. (Sonderausgabe zu Zwangsheirat und weiblicher Beschneidung)

Pandurang, Mala (2001): „How Sita and Deepak met. Helping German teenagers understand the Indian custom of ‚arranged marriages'", in: *Der Fremdsprachliche Unterricht Englisch,* Themenheft Indien", 2/2001, S. 41–43.

Oakland, John (2006[6]): *British Civilization. An Introduction.* London: Routledge.

Surkamp, Carola (2004): Teaching Films: Von der Filmanalyse zu handlungs- und prozessorientierten Formen der filmischen Textarbeit. In: *Der Fremdsprachliche Unterricht Englisch,* 68/2004, S. 2–13.

Stempleski, Susan/Barry Tomalin (2001): *Resource Books For Teachers. Film.* Oxford University Press. (mit vielen methodischen Anregungen)

Tepe, Thomas (Hrsg.) (2004): *Film im Englischunterricht. Filmanalyse. Vorschläge für Klausuren und Klassenarbeiten.* Stuttgart: Klett.

Tönnies, Merle/Claus-Ulrich Viol (Hg.) (2001): *British Political Speeches.* Stuttgart: Reclam, S. 63–84.

http://news.bbc.co.uk/hi/english/static/in_depth/uk/2002/race/generations.stm (längerer Artikel mit Audiointerview über eine multikulturelle Familie in Großbritannien → gekürzt als Klausur 2 im Heft)

http://news.bbc.co.uk/go/pr/fr/-/2/hi/south_asia/3191827.stm (Partnersuche und Heirat in Pakistan)

www.oiar.com/view_2635.htm (Erfahrungsaustausch über arrangierte Ehen)

www.f.waseda.jp/buda/texts/ballad.html (Ausführliche historisch und biographische Informationen zu Rudyard Kipling und u.a. eine Analyse seiner Ballade von Ost und West in einem Essay der *Otsuma Women's University Faculty* of *Literature Annual Report,* Vol. XVIII. No. 19, 1986)

www.weltwoche.ch/artikel/?AssetID=7578&CategoryID=60 (umfangreicher Essay zur Biografie von Rudyard Kipling vom Schriftsteller und Übersetzer Gisbert Haefs)
www.westernresistance.com/blog/archives/002234.html (Nachrichtensammlung zu Menschenrechtsverletzungen in verschiedenen Ländern, hier: Ehrenmorde, Verstümmelungen, Säureangriffe, Gruppenvergewaltigung von Frauen aufgrund alter Bräuche und fehlender Gesetzgebung)
http://whitewolf.newcastle.edu.au/words/authors/K/KiplingRudyard/verse/volumeXI/east-west.html (Ballad of East and West)
www.kipling.org.uk/bookmart_fra.htm (The Kipling Society)

(Alle angegebenen Internetquellen waren bis Mai 2008 verfügbar.)

Bildnachweis

S. 3, 18, 37, 38, 46, 51, 54, 55, 64, 68, 70, 88: ITN Source/Channel 4; S. 60: entnommen aus: Jane Walmsley: Brit-Think Ameri-Think. A Transatlantik Survival Guide. Edinburgh, Harrap 1986, S. 117; S. 63: © ullstein bild – KPA; S. 65: copyright © MGSpiller; S. 66: Lena Kara/Rex Features

Sollte trotz aller Bemühungen um korrekte Urheberangaben ein Irrtum unterlaufen sein, bitten wir darum, sich mit dem Verlag in Verbindung zu setzen, damit wir eventuell erforderliche Korrekturen vornehmen können.

EinFach Englisch

Unterrichtsmodelle

Herausgegeben von Hans Kröger

Ausgewählte Titel der Reihe:

Bend it Like Beckham
Filmanalyse
86 S., DIN A4, geh. Best.-Nr. 041212

Cultures in Conflict?
Literature on Ethnic Relationships
115 S., DIN A4, kart. Best.-Nr. 041220
Audio-CD: ca. 74 Min. Best.-Nr. 062407
Textausgabe: 148 S. Best.-Nr. 041218

Dead Poets Society
Filmanalyse
67 S., DIN A4, geh. Best.-Nr. 041255

East is East
Filmanalyse
102 S., DIN A4, geh. Best.-Nr. 041228

Echoes of the Empire. The Mixed Voices of a Colonial Past
20th Century English Short Stories
119 S., DIN A4, kart. Best.-Nr. 041223
Audio-CD: 78 Min. Best.-Nr. 062405
Textausgabe: 168 S. Best.-Nr. 041224

Forrest Gump
Filmanalyse
66 S., DIN A4, geh. Best.-Nr. 041231

Fried Green Tomatoes
Filmanalyse
136 S., DIN A4, kart. Best.-Nr. 041244

Poetry
104 S., DIN A4, kart. Best.-Nr. 041227

Political Speeches
Historical & Topical Issues
127 S., DIN A4, kart. Best.-Nr. 041236
Audio-CD: 70 Min. Best.-Nr. 062409
Textausgabe: 132 S. Best.-Nr. 041234

Rabbit-Proof Fence
Filmanalyse
54 S., DIN A4, geh. Best.-Nr. 041240

Tennessee Williams: A Streetcar Named Desire
90 S., DIN A4, geh. Best.-Nr. 041238

Strange Fruit and Other Songs
Cries for Social Consciousness and Civil Rights
59 S., mit Audio-CD,
DIN A4, geh. Best.-Nr. 041246

Urban Poetry
84 S., DIN A4, geh. Best.-Nr. 041232
Audio-CD: ca. 25 Min. Best.-Nr. 062413

Utopia and Dystopia
Exploring Alternative Worlds
92 S., DIN A4, kart. Best.-Nr. 041204
Textausgabe: 92 S. Best.-Nr. 041202

Paul Auster: Moon Palace
76 S., DIN A4, geh. Best.-Nr. 041226

Ray Bradbury: Fahrenheit 451
72 S., DIN A4, geh. Best.-Nr. 041214

Mark Haddon: The Curious Incident of the Dog in the Night-Time
99 S., DIN A4, kart. Best.-Nr. 041252

Lorraine Hansberry: A Raisin in the Sun
98 S., DIN A4, kart. Best.-Nr. 041241

Nick Hornby: About a Boy
inkl. Filmanalyse
93 S., DIN A4, kart. Best.-Nr. 041245

Aldous Huxley: Brave New World
93 S., DIN A4, kart. Best.-Nr. 041249

Ruth Prawer Jhabvala: Heat and Dust
87 S., DIN A4, geh. Best.-Nr. 041199

Harper Lee: To Kill a Mockingbird
108 S., DIN A4, kart. Best.-Nr. 041213

Ian McEwan: The Cement Garden
55 S., DIN A4, geh. Best.-Nr. 041251

Joyce Carol Oates: Big Mouth & Ugly Girl
84 S., DIN A4, geh. Best.-Nr. 041233

Meg Rosoff: How I Live Now
106 S., DIN A4, kart. Best.-Nr. 041253

Challenges – Global learning in a globalised world

Modelle und Methoden für den Englischunterricht

Herausgegeben von Engelbert Thaler

America's Global Role – Leader or Loner?
Von Iris Edelbrock und Andrea Schulz
78 S., 978-3-14-040206-4

Global Conflicts – Political Solutions
Von Martin Kohn
54 S., 978-3-14-040203-3

Global Warming – Earth's Climate at the Tipping Point?
Von Katharina Einhoff
62 S., 978-3-14-040201-9

The Changing Face of Multicultural Britain
Von Antje Blume
62 S., 978-3-14-040202-6

Popular Culture – Football, Films and Fashion
Von Engelbert Thaler
52 S., 978-3-14-040211-8

Science (Fiction) in the Third Millennium
Von Kirsten Pottbäcker
62 S., 978-3-14-040207-1

Terrorism – A Global Threat?
Von Patricia Anslinger und Gisa van Els
62 S., 978-3-14-040200-2

Global Economy – Hype, Hazard or Hope?
Von Iris Edelbrock und Birgit Schmidt-Grob
70 S., mit vierfarb. OH-Folien, 978-3-14-040209-5

Advertising and Marketing – Products, Promises and Persuasion
Von Iris Edelbrock und Birgit Schmidt-Grob
54 S., mit vierfarb. OH-Folien, 978-3-14-040210-1

Gender Matters – Exploring Male-Female Relationships
Von Engelbert Thaler
62 S., 978-3-14-040208-8

Them and US – On the Way to One World?
Von Katrin Kollmeyer
62 S., 978-3-14-040205-7

Source of Conflict or Recipe for Peace? – Religion in a Globalised World
Von Ulrich Schnakenberg
62 S., 978-3-14-040204-0

Weitere Titel sind in Vorbereitung.

Fordern Sie unseren Prospekt zur kompletten Reihe an:
Informationen zum Nulltarif ✆ 08 00 / 1 81 87 87

SCHÖNINGH VERLAG
Postfach 2540 · 33055 Paderborn

Schöningh

E-Mail: info@schoeningh.de
Internet: www.schoeningh-schulbuch.de